Answer the Call

be bold - evangelism workbook

Marie K. Diggs

ISBN: 979-8-9905573-1-4

Unless otherwise indicated, all Scripture quotations
are taken from the King James Version of the Bible.

Copyright © 2023 Marie Diggs Ministries - All rights reserved.
Unless otherwise indicated on specific pages, no portion of this manual may be reproduced, stored in a retrieval system, or transmitted in any form or by any means—electronic, mechanical, photocopy, recording or scanning, or other—except for brief quotation in critical reviews or articles, without prior written permission of the author.

MARIE DIGGS
MINISTRIES

P.O. Box 250471
West Bloomfield, MI 48325 • 248-990-0008
www.mariediggsministries.com

Table of Contents

Introduction v

Calendars vi

Evangelism Self-Assessment viii

▶ **Section 1: Understanding Evangelism**

    Chapter 1: What Is Evangelism? 2

    Chapter 2: Do I Have to Evangelize? 6

    Chapter 3: Why Evangelism? 10

    Chapter 4: Evangelism Through God's Eyes 14

    Chapter 5: Are Believers Evangelizing? 18

    Chapter 6: Evangelism Myths 22

    Chapter 7: Breaking the Spirit of Fear 26

▶ **Section 2: Salvation & Rededication**

    Chapter 8: What Is My Message? Understanding Salvation 34

    Chapter 9: Salvation Scriptures and Prayer for Evangelizing 40

    Chapter 10: Tips for Witnessing to the Unsaved 44

    Chapter 11: What Is My Message? Understanding Rededication 48

    Chapter 12: Rededication Scriptures and Prayer for Evangelizing 52

    Chapter 13: Tips for Witnessing to those Out of Fellowship & Backslidden 54

▶ **Section 3: Supernatural Help**

    Chapter 14: Evangelism Is About Partnership 60

    Chapter 15: Understanding Your Supernatural Equipment 64

▶ **Section 4: The Practical Side of Evangelism**

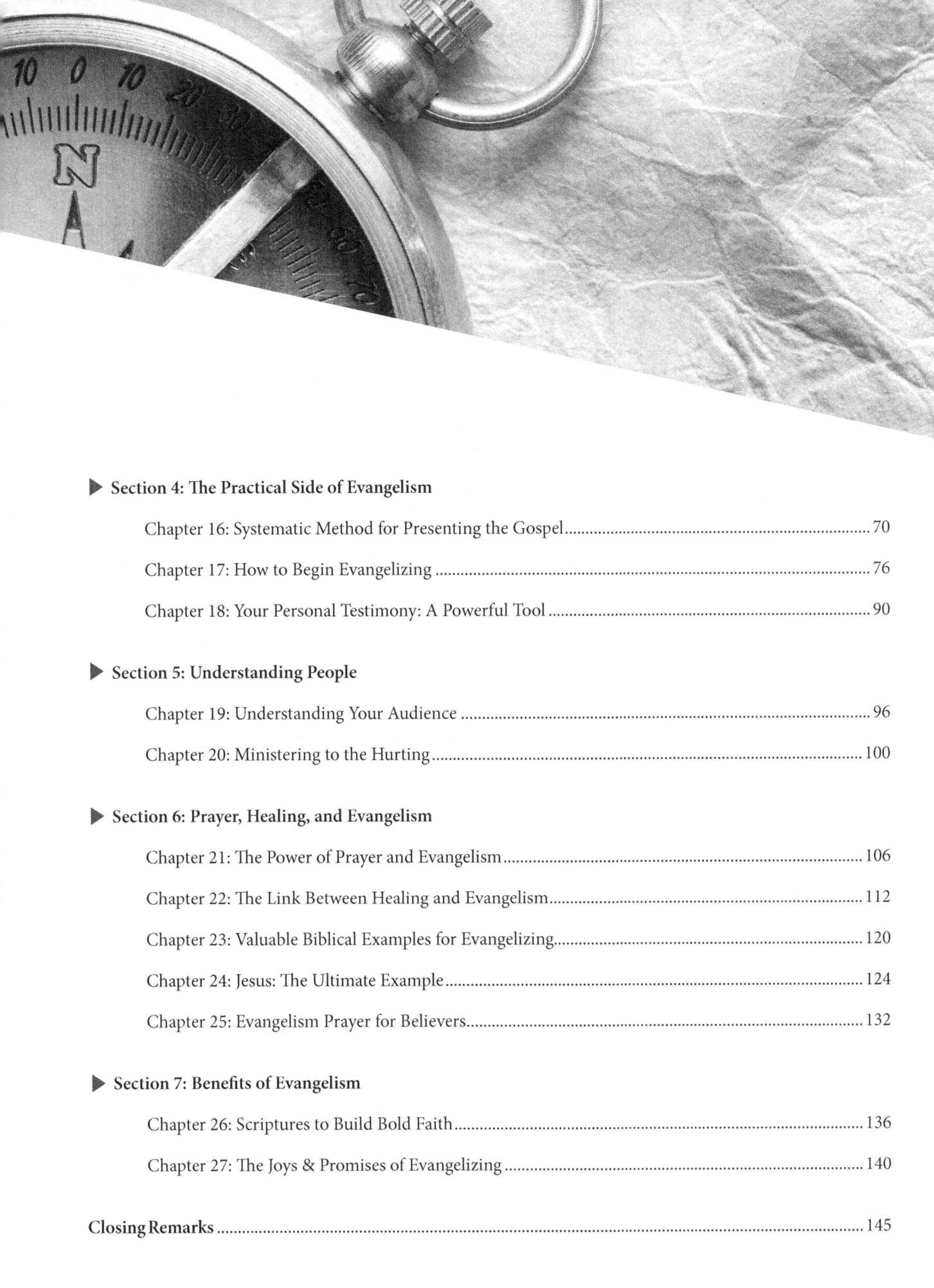

    Chapter 16: Systematic Method for Presenting the Gospel 70

    Chapter 17: How to Begin Evangelizing 76

    Chapter 18: Your Personal Testimony: A Powerful Tool 90

▶ **Section 5: Understanding People**

    Chapter 19: Understanding Your Audience 96

    Chapter 20: Ministering to the Hurting 100

▶ **Section 6: Prayer, Healing, and Evangelism**

    Chapter 21: The Power of Prayer and Evangelism 106

    Chapter 22: The Link Between Healing and Evangelism 112

    Chapter 23: Valuable Biblical Examples for Evangelizing 120

    Chapter 24: Jesus: The Ultimate Example 124

    Chapter 25: Evangelism Prayer for Believers 132

▶ **Section 7: Benefits of Evangelism**

    Chapter 26: Scriptures to Build Bold Faith 136

    Chapter 27: The Joys & Promises of Evangelizing 140

Closing Remarks 145

Answer the call

Introduction

The *Answer The Call: Be Bold - Evangelism Workbook* was developed from over thirty years of evangelism experience. Designed as an individualized learning tool to teach believers how to share Christ boldly and effectively without fear, the workbook aims to activate believers to fulfill their God-given mandate to multiply God's kingdom. It is a must-have for every believer.

When the proven principles in this manual are coupled with God's Word and put into action, lives will be changed, and eternities will be impacted!

Therefore, a commitment to studying this manual and choosing to live a life of evangelism is essential. Together, these two components pave the way for the power and the authority of Jesus to work in and through the believer's life, thereby changing the world—one person at a time (Acts 4:13).

How to Use This Workbook

This is a self-paced study that has been divided into twenty-seven chapters. This format lends well to completing the study in one month. For example, you may choose:

- **Day 1: Introduction and Evangelism Self-Assessment**
- **Days 2-29: Chapters 1-27**
- **Days 30-31: Review and Closing**

The workbook covers a lot of material, including Scriptures and suggestions for you to put your learning into practice. Therefore, you may choose to move through the workbook more slowly, and that is fine! Allow the Holy Spirit to be your guide for the study.

You Will Need

Using these items will help you get the most from this study:

- Bible (King James Version)
- Pen, pencil, highlighter pen
- Bible concordance; use this to define words and unfamiliar terms
- The Marie Diggs Ministries Be Bold app (download it at *www.beboldforjesus.com*)
- Multiple copies of the calendar templates on the next two pages. Several activities ask you to chart your progress or make reminders using a calendar. You can customize the templates and use them for these tasks.

Monthy Calendar

SUNDAY	MONDAY	TUESDAY	WEDNESDAY	THURSDAY	FRIDAY	SATURDAY

Permission granted to the purchaser of this workbook to photocopy this page for personal use.

Yearly Calendar

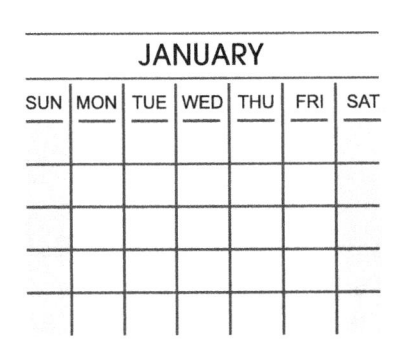

JANUARY	FEBRUARY	MARCH
SUN MON TUE WED THU FRI SAT	SUN MON TUE WED THU FRI SAT	SUN MON TUE WED THU FRI SAT

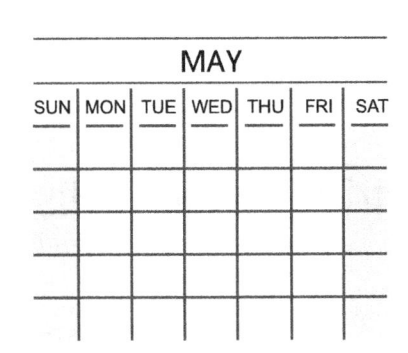

APRIL	MAY	JUNE
SUN MON TUE WED THU FRI SAT	SUN MON TUE WED THU FRI SAT	SUN MON TUE WED THU FRI SAT

JULY	AUGUST	SEPTEMBER
SUN MON TUE WED THU FRI SAT	SUN MON TUE WED THU FRI SAT	SUN MON TUE WED THU FRI SAT

OCTOBER	NOVEMBER	DECEMBER
SUN MON TUE WED THU FRI SAT	SUN MON TUE WED THU FRI SAT	SUN MON TUE WED THU FRI SAT

Permission granted to the purchaser of this workbook to photocopy this page for personal use.

Evangelism Self-Assessment

Below is an Evangelism Self-Assessment. Complete the assessment by answering the questions as honestly as possible. Print a copy of the self-assessment, fill it out, and keep it with this workbook or with your Bible.

Next, set a reminder on your phone or calendar for six months from today. After you've completed the workbook and put into practice what you've learned, take this self-assessment again. Note how much you've grown and how God is working in and through you! Revisit this self-assessment periodically to monitor your progress.

Marie Diggs Ministries Evangelism Self-Assessment

MDM's Assessment is only to assist you in realizing your growth while learning from the Evangelism Workbook.

FIRST NAME:

TODAY'S DATE:

LAST NAME:

YOUR TITLE:

ASSESS YOUR CURRENT LEVEL OF COMFORT AND SKILL WHEN IT RELATES TO...	HIGH COMFORT	SOME COMFORT	NOT COMFORTABLE
SHARING THE GOSPEL OF JESUS CHRIST WITH OTHERS			
SHARING THE PLAN OF SALVATION WITH OTHERS			
PRAYING ALOUD WITH OTHERS			
PROVIDING SCRIPTURAL REFERENCES (BOOK AND VERSE)			
MINISTERING SALVATION AND/OR RE-DEDICATION TO OTHERS			
EXPLAINING RE-DEDICATION TO THOSE WHO HAVE BACKSLIDDEN			
LISTENING AND IDENTIFYING WHERE OTHERS ARE SPIRITUALLY			
APPROACHING OTHERS TO SHARE THE GOSPEL (STRANGERS, CO-WORKERS, ETC.)			

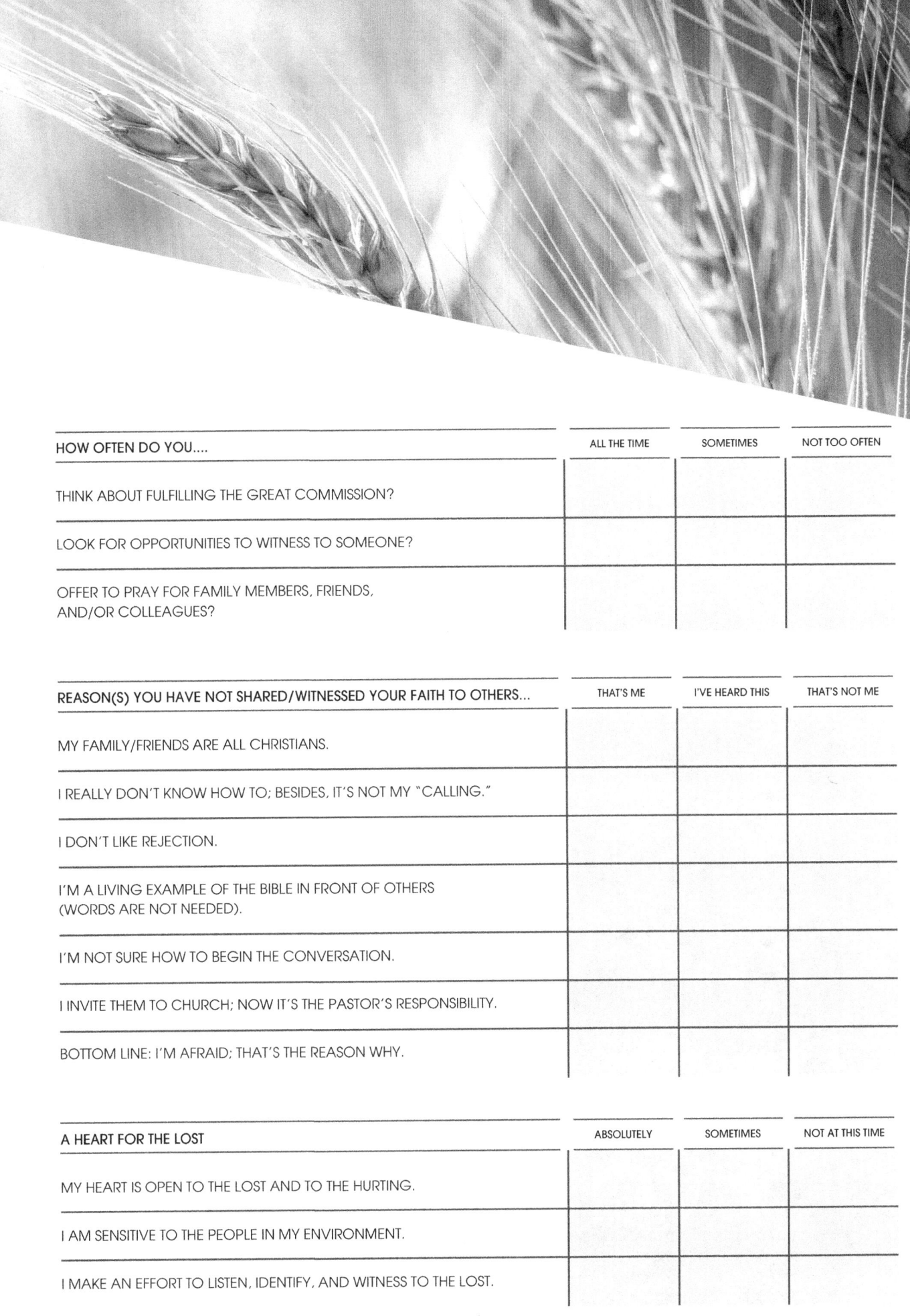

HOW OFTEN DO YOU….	ALL THE TIME	SOMETIMES	NOT TOO OFTEN
THINK ABOUT FULFILLING THE GREAT COMMISSION?			
LOOK FOR OPPORTUNITIES TO WITNESS TO SOMEONE?			
OFFER TO PRAY FOR FAMILY MEMBERS, FRIENDS, AND/OR COLLEAGUES?			

REASON(S) YOU HAVE NOT SHARED/WITNESSED YOUR FAITH TO OTHERS…	THAT'S ME	I'VE HEARD THIS	THAT'S NOT ME
MY FAMILY/FRIENDS ARE ALL CHRISTIANS.			
I REALLY DON'T KNOW HOW TO; BESIDES, IT'S NOT MY "CALLING."			
I DON'T LIKE REJECTION.			
I'M A LIVING EXAMPLE OF THE BIBLE IN FRONT OF OTHERS (WORDS ARE NOT NEEDED).			
I'M NOT SURE HOW TO BEGIN THE CONVERSATION.			
I INVITE THEM TO CHURCH; NOW IT'S THE PASTOR'S RESPONSIBILITY.			
BOTTOM LINE: I'M AFRAID; THAT'S THE REASON WHY.			

A HEART FOR THE LOST	ABSOLUTELY	SOMETIMES	NOT AT THIS TIME
MY HEART IS OPEN TO THE LOST AND TO THE HURTING.			
I AM SENSITIVE TO THE PEOPLE IN MY ENVIRONMENT.			
I MAKE AN EFFORT TO LISTEN, IDENTIFY, AND WITNESS TO THE LOST.			

Understanding Evangelism

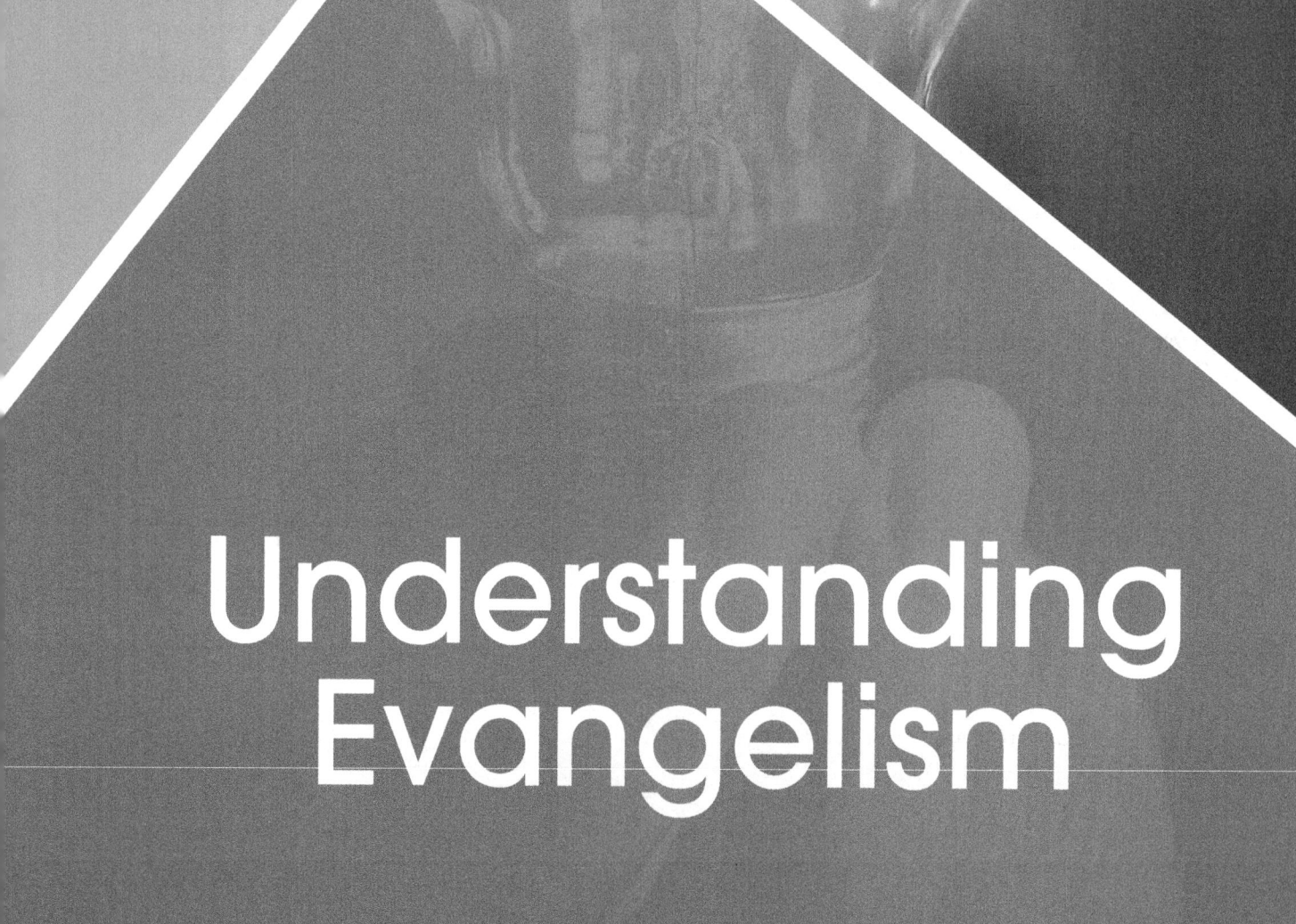

In this Section:

▶ **What Is Evangelism?**
Evangelism is the spreading of the good news of the Gospel of Jesus Christ.

▶ **Do I Have to Evangelize?**
Spreading the Gospel of Jesus Christ is not a suggestion. It is a direct command given to believers from God.

▶ **Why Evangelism?**
It's a matter of family! God has commanded believers to evangelize because He wants His family back!

▶ **Evangelism Through God's Eyes**
Evangelism is the first assignment given to every believer after they become saved.

▶ **Are Believers Evangelizing?**
Various groups were asked: "When was the last time a person approached you, witnessed to you, and attempted to lead you into salvation or rededication?"

▶ **Evangelism Myths**
Truth vs. Myth: How do these changes impact your attitude about sharing the Gospel of Jesus Christ?

▶ **Breaking the Spirit of Fear**
Most believers do not evangelize due to being gripped by fear. Fear stops the believer from acting on God's Word.

Chapter 1
What Is Evangelism?

Evangelism is the spreading of the good news of the Gospel of Jesus Christ.

This includes:

- **Preaching**: Proclaiming a clear and detailed message of the life, death, and resurrection of Jesus Christ and the way to salvation through Him.
- **Communicating**: Sharing or exchanging information regarding the life, death, and resurrection of Jesus Christ and the way to salvation through Him.
- **Promoting**: Furthering and advancing the cause and progress of the Gospel.

Evangelism should be a way of life for every believer. It should be so ingrained in them that it is like breathing.

Many believers have the wrong outlook regarding evangelism. They see it as an insurmountable, overwhelming task of which they are afraid, and they don't have the time or the skills to do.

Some Reasons Why Believers Have This Outlook

Read the points below and circle the reasons that apply to you.

- ▶ Pure Fear
- ▶ Lack of Knowledge
- ▶ Identity Crisis
- ▶ Uncaring Attitude (regarding non-believers)

In the space below, journal a few thoughts about why you have this outlook regarding evangelism.

The points listed above should never stop believers from sharing the truth of God's love with others. Paul said it this way: Believers must not be ashamed of God's good news, which is Jesus, Himself! The good news is that God has sent Jesus to rescue mankind from sin, the effects of sin, and from Satan (see Romans 1:15-16).

In addition, the good news is that everyone who receives Jesus as Lord and Savior becomes a partaker of the blessing of Abraham as seen in the book of Galatians.

Read Galatians 3:6-14, 26-29.
In the space below, write down the blessings of being an heir of Abraham:

Chapter 1
What is Evangelism?

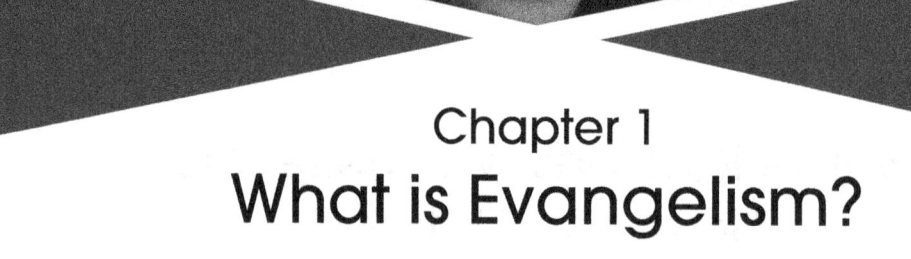

1. What are two reasons why believers have the wrong outlook regarding evangelism?

2. What three ways do believers spread the good news (the Gospel of Jesus Christ)?

3. Everyone who receives Jesus is a partaker of what?

4. To be ashamed of the good news is to be ashamed of whom?

5. What is evangelism?

6. In receiving Jesus as Lord and Savior, mankind is rescued from what three things?

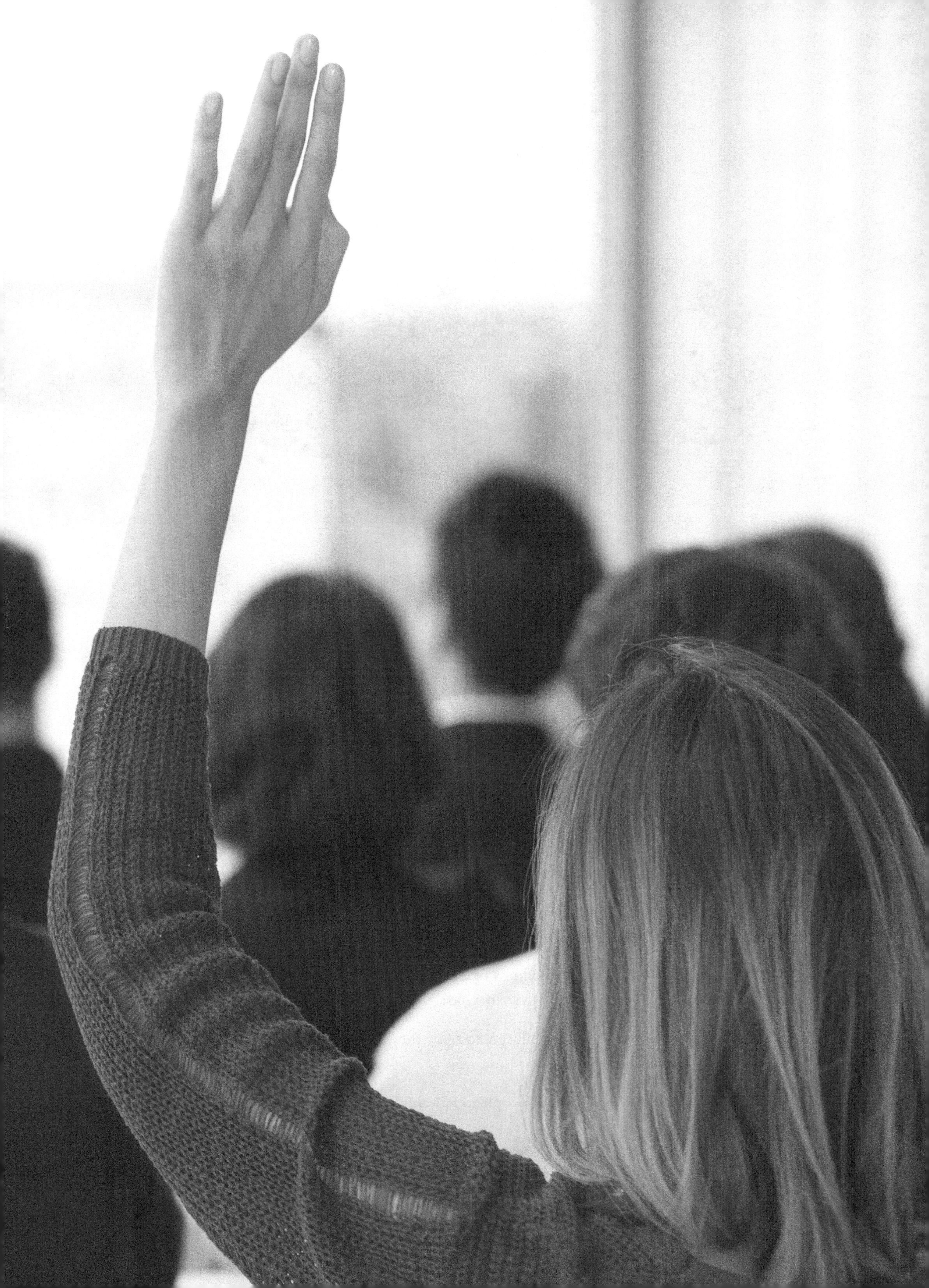

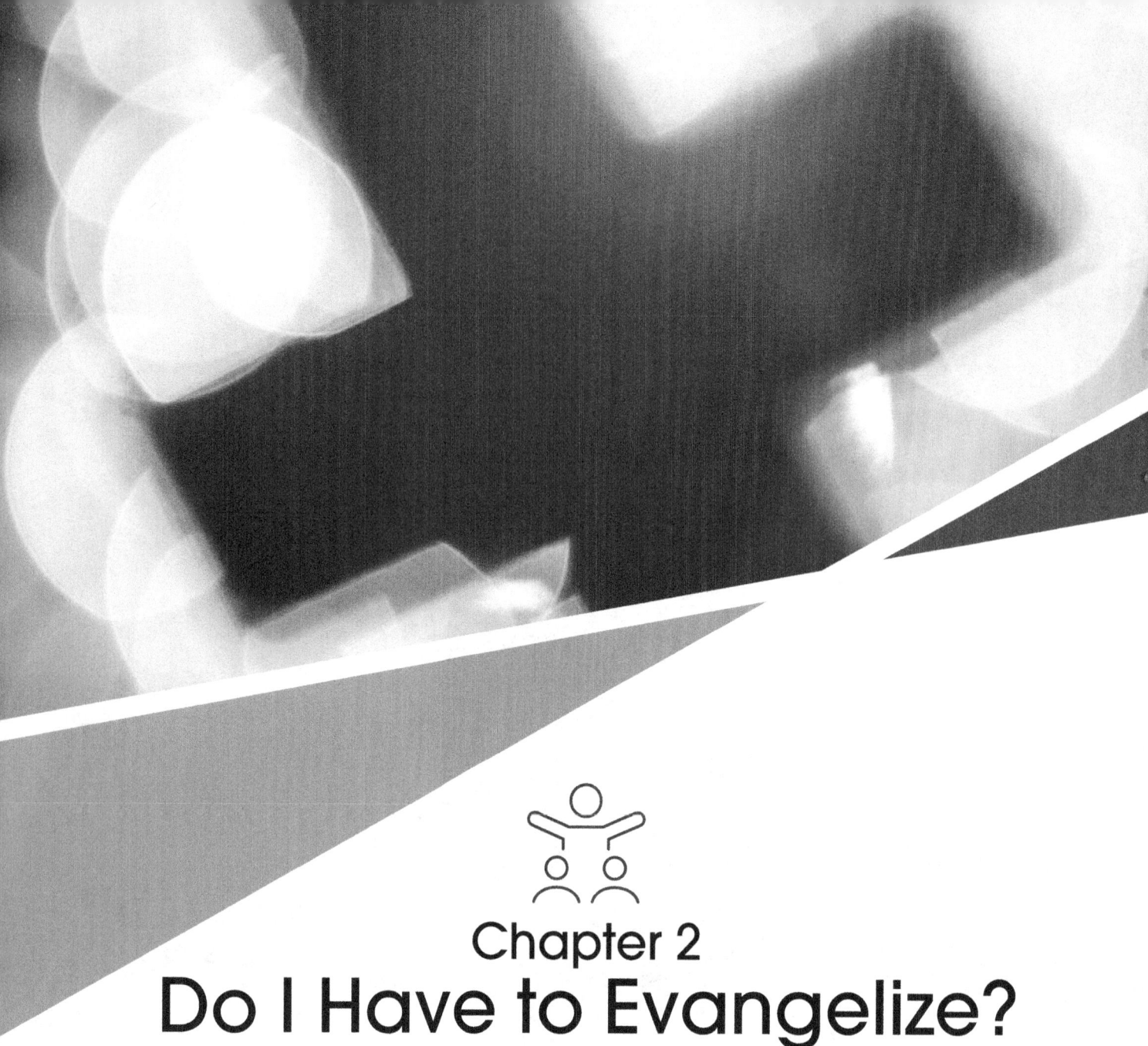

Chapter 2
Do I Have to Evangelize?

Spreading the Gospel of Jesus Christ is not a suggestion. It is a direct command given to believers from God.

▶ The command to evangelize was given to everyone who would come to believe upon Jesus Christ and receive Him as their Lord and Savior.

▶ Every believer who has tasted the goodness of God by receiving His Son Jesus as their Lord and Savior has a responsibility to evangelize and to share God's goodness with others.

▶ God expects believers, who are His children, to show they are equipped to do the work of the ministry and to participate in making Him rich.

▶ God has entrusted the eternal lives of people to His children, and He expects believers to be imitators of Him.

Scriptures Regarding Evangelism Being a Command

Read the following Scriptures. Circle any important words or phrases in each passage.

Matthew 24:14
And this gospel of the kingdom shall be preached in all the world for a witness unto all nations; and then shall the end come.

Matthew 28:18-20
And Jesus came and spake unto them, saying, All power is given unto me in heaven and in earth. Go ye therefore, and teach all nations, baptizing them in the name of the Father, and of the Son, and of the Holy Ghost: Teaching them to observe all things whatsoever I have commanded you: and, lo, I am with you always, even unto the end of the world. Amen.

Mark 16:15-20
And he said unto them, Go ye into all the world, and preach the gospel to every creature. He that believeth and is baptized shall be saved; but he that believeth not shall be damned. And these signs shall follow them that believe; In my name shall they cast out devils; they shall speak with new tongues; They shall take up serpents; and if they drink any deadly thing, it shall not hurt them; they shall lay hands on the sick, and they shall recover. So then after the Lord had spoken unto them, he was received up into heaven, and sat on the right hand of God. And they went forth, and preached every where, the Lord working with *them*, and confirming the word with signs following. Amen.

Luke 24:45-49
Then opened he their understanding, that they might understand the scriptures, And said unto them, Thus it is written, and thus it behooved Christ to suffer, and to rise from the dead the third day: And that repentance and remission of sins should be preached in his name among all nations, beginning at Jerusalem. And ye are witnesses of these things. And, behold, I send the promise of my Father upon you: but tarry ye in the city of Jerusalem, until ye be endued with power from on high.

John 17:20-21
Neither pray I for these alone, but for them also which shall believe on me through their word; That they all may be one; as thou, Father, art in me, and I in thee, that they also may be one in us: that the world may believe that thou hast sent me.

John 20:19-23

Then the same day at evening, being the first day of the week, when the doors were shut where the disciples were assembled for fear of the Jews, came Jesus and stood in the midst, and saith unto them, Peace be unto you. And when he had so said, he shewed unto them his hands and his side. Then were the disciples glad, when they saw the LORD. Then said Jesus to them again, Peace be unto you: as my Father hath sent me, even so send I you. And when he had said this, he breathed on them, and saith unto them, Receive ye the Holy Ghost: Whose soever sins ye remit, they are remitted unto them; and whose soever sins ye retain, they are retained.

Acts 1:8-9

But ye shall receive power, after that the Holy Ghost is come upon you: and ye shall be witnesses unto me both in Jerusalem, and in all Judaea, and in Samaria, and unto the uttermost part of the earth. And when he had spoken these things, while they beheld, he was taken up; and a cloud received him out of their sight.

2 Corinthians 5:17-21

Therefore if any man be in Christ, he is a new creature: old things are passed away; behold, all things are become new. And all things are of God, who hath reconciled us to himself by Jesus Christ, and hath given to us the ministry of reconciliation; To wit, that God was in Christ, reconciling the world unto himself, not imputing their trespasses unto them; and hath committed unto us the word of reconciliation. Now then we are ambassadors for Christ, as though God did beseech you by us: we pray you in Christ's stead, be ye reconciled to God. For he hath made him to be sin for us, who knew no sin; that we might be made the righteousness of God in him.

In the space below, journal your feelings about God's requirement of you.

Chapter 2
Do I Have to Evangelize?

1. Believers are to make obvious that they are equipped to take part in making God rich. How do believers make God rich?

2. What does the Lord require of believers according to Matthew 28:18-20 and Mark 16:15-20?

3. Spreading the Gospel of Jesus Christ is a _____ to believers from God.

4. God expects His children to be _____

5. What is your answer to the question in this chapter's title (do I have to evangelize)?

Chapter 3
Why Evangelize?

It's a matter of family! God has commanded believers to evangelize because He wants His family back! He longs for everyone in the world to know His love and to receive the gift of His Son, Jesus.

This truth makes evangelism much more than a "command" from God. It is the vehicle that He has chosen to use to increase His family! When Christians adopt God's attitude about evangelism, they truly see through the eyes of God.

Scriptural Truths That Emphasize God's Desire for Family

Read the following Scriptures. Circle any important words or phrases in each passage.

John 1:12-13
But as many as received him, to them gave he power to become the sons of God, even to them that believe on his name: Which were born, not of blood, nor of the will of the flesh, nor of the will of man, but of God.

Romans 8:15-17
For ye have not received the spirit of bondage again to fear; but ye have received the Spirit of adoption, whereby we cry, Abba, Father. The Spirit itself beareth witness with our spirit, that we are the children of God: And if children, then heirs; heirs of God, and joint-heirs with Christ; if so be that we suffer with him, that we may be also glorified together.

Ephesians 1:4-5
According as he hath chosen us in him before the foundation of the world, that we should be holy and without blame before him in love: Having predestinated us unto the adoption of children by Jesus Christ to himself, according to the good pleasure of his will...

Ephesians 2:12-19
That at that time ye were without Christ, being aliens from the commonwealth of Israel, and strangers from the covenants of promise, having no hope, and without God in the world: But now in Christ Jesus ye who sometimes were far off are made nigh by the blood of Christ. For he is our peace, who hath made both one, and hath broken down the middle wall of partition between us; Having abolished in his flesh the enmity, even the law of commandments contained in ordinances; for to make in himself of twain one new man, so making peace; And that he might reconcile both unto God in one body by the cross, having slain the enmity thereby: And came and preached peace to you which were afar off, and to them that were nigh. For through him we both have access by one Spirit unto the Father. Now therefore ye are no more strangers and foreigners, but fellow citizens with the saints, and of the household of God;...

Ephesians 3:14-15
For this cause I bow my knees unto the Father of our Lord Jesus Christ, Of whom the whole family in heaven and earth is named,...

Ephesians 5:1
Be ye therefore followers of God, as dear children;...

1 John 3:1-2
Behold, what manner of love the Father hath bestowed upon us, that we should be called the sons of God: therefore the world knoweth us not, because it knew him not. Beloved, now are we the sons of God, and it doth not yet appear what we shall be: but we know that, when he shall appear, we shall be like him; for we shall see him as he is.

In the space below, journal about how these Scriptures make you feel as a member of God's family.

Read the genealogy of Jesus in Luke 3:23-38.
Then write down your thoughts about the first man Adam being the "son of God."

Chapter 3
Why Evangelism?

1. In addition to evangelism being a command, what else is it?

2. God longs for _____ to know His love and receive the gift of His Son, Jesus.

3. God has commanded believers to evangelize because He wants

4. What happens to Christians when they adopt God's attitude about evangelism?

Chapter 4
Evangelism Through God's Eyes

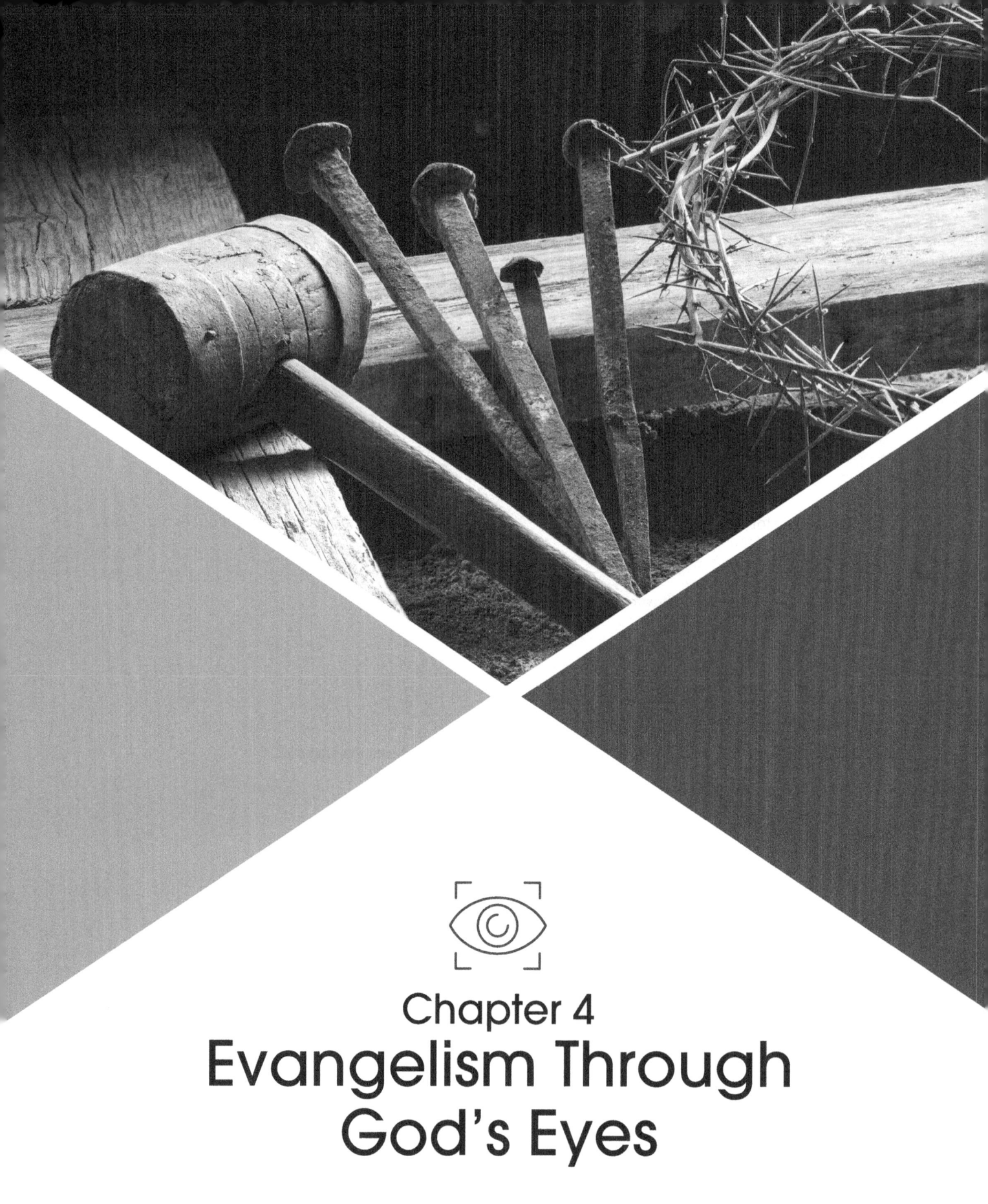

Evangelism is the first assignment given to every believer after they become saved. Yes, that's right. God expects new believers to tell others about His good news, the gift of Jesus! Therefore, evangelism comes easy for believers because they were born to do it.

Evangelism from God's Point of View

Read 2 Corinthians 5:17-20, and as you consider evangelism from God's point of view, meditate on the confidence that God has in you to fulfill His will:

- ▶ God is not unjust. Therefore, He would never command believers to carry out an assignment that they could not successfully accomplish.

- ▶ God commanded every believer to share the Gospel. He has faith in the ability He has placed in them and upon them to share the Gospel. God has given every believer a message with the right words to say; they just need to share it.

- ▶ God has given every believer the ministry of reconciliation (or restoration). Therefore, no believer should be waiting to serve God. They should be actively serving Him with the first ministry given to them upon receiving salvation.

- ▶ God has committed or obligated every believer unto the word of reconciliation, and He expects loyalty to His assignment.

- ▶ God has given every believer the title of "ambassador for Christ" because He has chosen to commit and obligate them to the word of reconciliation.

- ▶ God needs believers to witness for Christ. God knows that non-believers can't evangelize because they haven't experienced salvation or a life with Jesus.

- ▶ God invites non-believers to receive salvation through His Son, Jesus Christ, by using believers as His mouthpiece and exhibitors of His power.

> *"When we choose to see everyone through the eyes of God,
> then we will see everyone through the eyes of love."*
> —Evangelist Marie Diggs

Chapter 4
Evangelism Through God's Eyes

1. When is the assignment given to every believer?

2. Why does evangelism come easy for every believer?

3. What has God given to every believer?

4. What is the first ministry given to the believer upon receiving salvation?

5. Who does God use as His mouthpiece?

6. How does God invite non-believers to receive salvation?

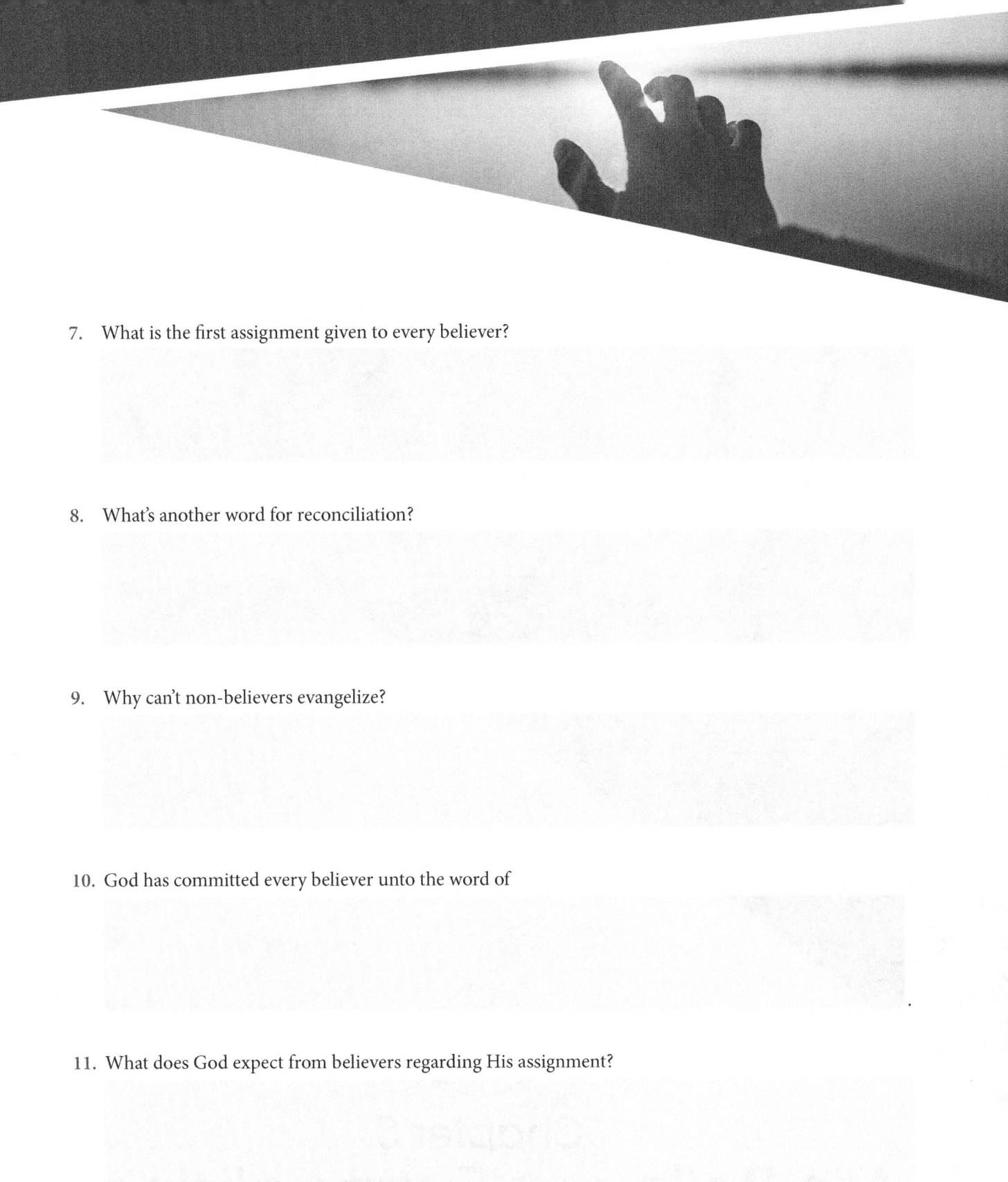

7. What is the first assignment given to every believer?

8. What's another word for reconciliation?

9. Why can't non-believers evangelize?

10. God has committed every believer unto the word of

11. What does God expect from believers regarding His assignment?

12. What title has God given to every believer?

Chapter 5
Are Believers Evangelizing?

Throughout 2017, Marie Diggs Ministries (MDM) conducted multiple evangelism conferences and ministry engagements within the United States and one overseas. The various groups of people were asked the following question: "When was the last time a person approached you with the full Gospel message, witnessed to you, and attempted to lead you into salvation or rededication?"

Summary of Responses to Our Poll

▶ Most people polled signified that they had not been approached within ten years or more.

▶ A vast number of believers are not evangelizing.

▶ In the last ten to fifteen years, there has been a drastic decline in the number of churches that equip the body of Christ in their congregation to evangelize.

▶ Many churches claim to evangelize in other nations but struggle to reach people in America.

▶ Evangelism has become a lost art.

Instead of focusing on why believers are not evangelizing, let's focus on equipping and mobilizing the body of Christ.

Among Churchgoers

In the past six months, how many times did you share with someone how to become a Christian?

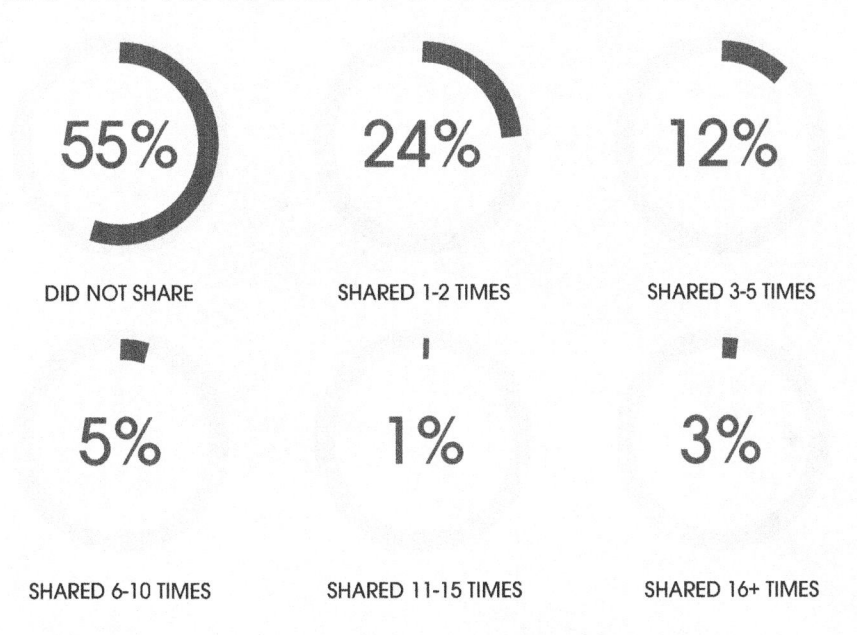

55% DID NOT SHARE

24% SHARED 1-2 TIMES

12% SHARED 3-5 TIMES

5% SHARED 6-10 TIMES

1% SHARED 11-15 TIMES

3% SHARED 16+ TIMES

Reference: Lifeway Research (2023). *Fast Facts*. Lifeway Research, a ministry of Lifeway Christian Resources; Nashville, TN. https://research.lifeway.com/fast-facts

Activate Your Circle of People to Evangelize by Taking a Poll

List your believing family members, friends, and acquaintances whom you plan to approach with a poll. Record their responses and check them off the list once you have spoken with them.

- ▶ Ask them to honestly share with you the last time that they've shared the Gospel leading someone either into salvation or rededication.

- ▶ Do not condemn them if they have never evangelized or haven't done it in a while.

- ▶ Encourage them to step up and begin to evangelize.

- ▶ Allow your lifestyle of evangelism to inspire them.

There is much work for believers to do. Jesus is waiting on believers everywhere to take up the mantle that He left for them to enlarge God's family!

Mark 16:15
"…Go ye into all the world, and preach the gospel to every creature."

Prayerfully ask the Holy Spirit to help you to be obedient to this scripture.

Chapter 5
Are Believers Evangelizing?

1. What does Mark 16:15 instruct believers to do?

2. Per MDM's poll regarding the above question, most people had not been approached within how many years?

3. Are a vast number of believers evangelizing?

4. Based on the results of MDM's poll, evangelism has become a   .

5. Has there been a decline in the number of people evangelizing over the past ten to fifteen years?

6. What has been the state of the church over the past ten to fifteen years regarding equipping the body of Christ to evangelize?

7. When was the last time someone approached you with the full Gospel message, witnessed to you, and attempted to lead you into salvation or rededication?

Chapter 6
Evangelism Myths

As you read through the myths regarding evangelism, check each box that best describes some of your attitudes regarding sharing Christ. Then write down how each truth for the myth that you checked changes your attitude about sharing Christ.

✔	MYTH	TRUTH	HOW MY ATTITUDE IS CHANGED?
	I don't have the personality to evangelize.	God wouldn't give a person a personality that hinders His assignment or plan for their life.	
	I'm shy and not bold enough to evangelize.	God has not given believers the spirit of fear. The righteous are as bold as lions.	
	It's my pastor's or minister's responsibility.	God has given every believer the ministry of reconciliation and has committed unto every believer the word of reconciliation.	
	I do community work, so I'm evangelizing.	Community work is important and has its place in expressing the love of God to people. Community work should not replace witnessing; it should complement it!	
	I serve in my church; I don't need to evangelize.	Every believer should serve in their local church, and every believer should also obey God's command to evangelize and share Christ.	
	I invite people to church.	Inviting people to church is great; however, it does not fulfill the command to evangelize.	

✔	MYTH	TRUTH	HOW MY ATTITUDE IS CHANGED?
	I pray for people to get saved.	Praying is great. It softens hearts to receive from God and makes believers more sensitive to God's voice, but it doesn't replace the command to evangelize.	
	I pass out tracts.	Providing people with more information while evangelizing is great. However, distributing tracts without evangelizing hinders the believer from allowing God to utilize them as a mouthpiece. (The exception to this would be if a person was not at liberty to engage in personal conversations, such as while working on their company's time.)	
	My life is a witness for Christ.	Every believer's life should be a witness for Christ. When a believer's attitude is that their life is a witness for Christ, then that believer should be more compelled to evangelize, due to his or her closeness and walk with God. After all, Jesus' life on Earth was an example. Although Jesus was sinless, God still saw the need for Him to evangelize His message.	
	I'm waiting for the Holy Spirit to lead me.	Evangelism is a command; like walking in love with people is a command. Most believers don't wait for the Holy Spirit to tell them to walk in love with a person, because walking in love is a known command that believers strive to adhere to. Evangelism is a command, too. Believers must renew their minds to embrace and obey this command.	
	I'm not a "people person."	People have different dispositions; however, that does not negate God's command to evangelize.	
	People don't want to hear the Gospel.	There will always be people who are not open to hear the Gospel message. That should not hinder believers from actively sharing the Gospel of Christ because it is the power of God unto salvation.	

Believers can no longer allow the above-mentioned myths to stop them from evangelizing. God gave Jesus a message to proclaim while He lived on the Earth, and God has given believers a message to proclaim while they live on the Earth also. Jesus and believers have been given *the same* message and spiritual equipment. The only missing ingredient is *the same* obedience.

Be encouraged. Jesus said in **John 14:12:** "Verily, verily, I say unto you, He that believeth on me, the works that I do shall he do also; and greater works than these shall he do; because I go unto my Father."

> *"As members of the Body of Christ, we have been enlisted and supernaturally empowered to work with Jesus and to finish His work on the Earth. Let's not put Jesus in an unemployment line because we are not doing the work!"*
>
> —Evangelist Marie Diggs

Chapter 6
Evangelism Myths

1. Write out John 14:12 on the lines below and then memorize it.

2. Why is community work not evangelizing?

3. Is praying for people or passing out tracts a good substitute for evangelizing?

4. Although a believer's life might be a witness for Christ, why should they still be more compelled to evangelize?

5. Why is "I'm waiting for the Holy Spirit to lead me" not a good defense for *not* evangelizing?

6. Jesus and believers have been given the same message and the same spiritual equipment. What is the only missing ingredient?

7. Why is it an error to think or say, "I don't have the personality to evangelize, or I'm not a 'people person'?"

Chapter 7
Breaking the Spirit of Fear

Most believers do not evangelize due to being gripped by the spirit of fear. Fear stops the believer from acting on God's Word. Fear should not dominate or control a believer's life or decisions. Fear should be inferior to every believer, and every believer should be superior to fear!

When a believer's life is controlled by fear, that believer:

- ▶ Is experiencing an identity crisis—not knowing who they are in Christ
- ▶ Has failed to realize that they are seated in heavenly places with Christ Jesus
- ▶ Has given the Devil an opportunity in their life (see Ephesians 4:27)
- ▶ Has taken a spirit that God has not given them

Read 2 Timothy 1:7 and define the words *power*, *love*, and *a sound mind* using a Bible concordance. Then write down why it is important that the spirit of fear is broken off every believer.

Read James 2:19, and you will find that the devils are afraid of God and that they believe in Him.

The Devil knows who God is, and he also knows that he is subject to God. But he is also subject to you! Remember what Jesus said in **Luke 10:19-20.**

"Behold, I give unto you power to tread on serpents and scorpions, and over all the power of the enemy: and nothing shall by any means hurt you. Notwithstanding in this rejoice not, that the spirits are subject unto you; but rather rejoice, that your names are written in heaven."

These verses should cause boldness to arise in your heart because you have been authorized to trample over your enemy without him having the authority to harm you. No fear here!

Satan's Purpose for Using the Spirit of Fear

Place a check by each point where the spirit of fear has manifested and is trying to remain in your life.

✓	Personal Self-Assessment
	To stop you from realizing your true identity
	To stop you from operating in the authority and power that you possess
	To control your thought processes
	To stop you from obeying God's command to evangelize
	To stop you from being freed from sin and from Satan's dominion
	To ultimately dominate your life

Reflect on how Satan uses the spirit of fear to hurt God by paralyzing God's people, which causes them not to witness, which, in turn means that non-believers live without God in this life and face an eternal future without Him.

Use the space below to journal your thoughts.

Principles to Break Free from The Spirit of Fear

Personal Action Tasks: Each point requires a decision from you. Use the blank monthly calendar template to chart your progress. Customize it for your use. Record on the calendar when you complete each point below. Celebrate your accomplishments.

- ▶ Read James 4:7
- ▶ Decide to be free from fear.
- ▶ Solidify your decision by daily meditating on the Scriptures found in this section of the manual.
- ▶ Read the Scriptures aloud slowly and think about what you are saying.
- ▶ Choose to agree with God's Word regarding your situation.
- ▶ Take your freedom from fear by faith being fully persuaded and assured that you have what God's Word says about you.
- ▶ Thank God daily that you are free from the spirit of fear.
- ▶ Change your speech. No longer say, "I'm afraid" or "I'm scared to evangelize."
- ▶ Find a way to act on your faith in God's Word.

Be aware that Satan will come to see if you really believe God's Word. Be prepared to resist him and to reject his lies and lying imaginations. Only speak what the Word of God says about you. No longer allow yourself to be enslaved by the spirit of fear. Stay free!

As you meditate on the truth of God's Word, it will become firmly planted in your heart, causing you, as an ambassador for Christ, to evangelize boldly and confidently.

NO WORD = NO FAITH = NO ACTION!
Scriptures to Meditate On to Stay Free from Fear

Psalm 118:6
The LORD is on my side; I will not fear: what can man do unto me?

Proverbs 28:1
The wicked flee when no man pursueth: but the righteous are bold as a lion.

Romans 8:15
For ye have not received the spirit of bondage again to fear; but ye have received the Spirit of adoption, whereby we cry, Abba, Father.

Philippians 1:14
And many of the brethren in the Lord, waxing confident by my bonds, are much more bold to speak the word without fear.

Hebrews 13:6
So that we may boldly say, The Lord is my helper, and I will not fear what man shall do unto me.

1 John 4:18
There is no fear in love; but perfect love casteth out fear: because fear hath torment. He that feareth is not made perfect in love.

Scriptures to Combat Fear Within Your Mind

2 Corinthians 10:3-5
For though we walk in the flesh, we do not war after the flesh: (For the weapons of our warfare are not carnal, but mighty through God to the pulling down of strong holds;) Casting down imaginations, and every high thing that exalteth itself against the knowledge of God, and bringing into captivity every thought to the obedience of Christ;...

Philippians 4:6-8
Be careful for nothing; but in every thing by prayer and supplication with thanksgiving let your requests be made known unto God. And the peace of God, which passeth all understanding, shall keep your hearts and minds through Christ Jesus. Finally, brethren, whatsoever things are true, whatsoever things are honest, whatsoever things are just, whatsoever things are pure, whatsoever things are lovely, whatsoever things are of good report; if there be any virtue, and if there be any praise, think on these things.

Philippians 4:13
I can do all things through Christ which strengtheneth me.

> *"Satan is afraid. After all, after the fall of Adam and Eve in the book of Genesis, Satan's nature immediately manifested in them when they hid themselves from God in the Garden of Eden because they were afraid. As a Christian, you no longer have Satan's nature. Therefore, no more hiding!"*
>
> —Evangelist Marie Diggs

Chapter 7
Breaking the Spirit of Fear

1. Write out two Scriptures to combat fear:

2. Second Timothy 1:7 documents that believers are superior to fear. What does it say?

3. List four results of a believer being gripped by the spirit of fear.

4. Why is it that most believers do not evangelize?

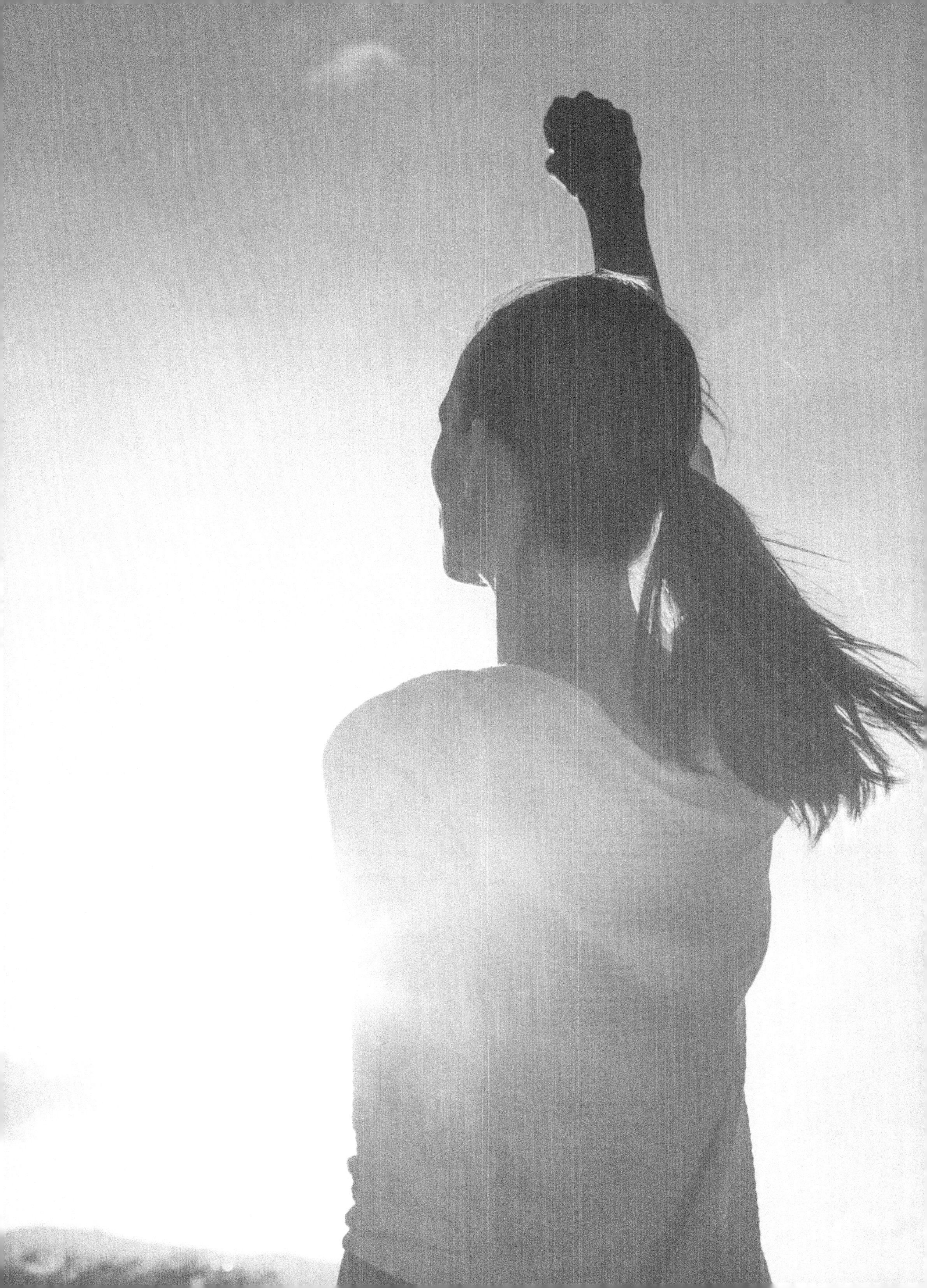

Salvation & Rededication

In this Section:

▶ **What Is My Message?**
Understanding Salvation
"I am under the impression that it is not that people don't want to receive Jesus, but that they just don't know enough about Him!" - *Marie Diggs*

▶ **Salvation Scriptures and Prayer for Evangelizing**
As you memorize scripture, God's Word will flow from your spirit with ease while evangelizing

▶ **Tips for Witnessing to the Unsaved**
A series of tips you can begin to incorporate into your witnessing opportunities with the Unsaved

▶ **What Is My Message?**
Understanding Rededication
"As Christians, we should fervently go after our backslidden and out-of-fellowship brothers and sisters instead of leaving them hurt on the battlefield." - *Marie Diggs*

▶ **Rededication Scriptures and Prayer for Evangelizing**
Scriptures and rededication Prayer that you can use to lead someone back into fellowship with God

▶ **Tips for Witnessing to Out-of-Fellowship & Backslidden**
A series of tips you can begin to incorporate into your witnessing opportunities with the Out-of-Fellowship and Backslidden.

Chapter 8
What Is My Message?
Understanding Salvation

Read every Scripture and the scriptural enlightenments. Meditate on God's messages in each passage. You'll find all the Scriptures from this chapter printed without commentary in the next chapter. That list will be a helpful tool for meditation and memorization.

The Sin Issue

Wherefore, as by one man sin entered into the world, and death by sin; and so death passed upon all men, for that all have sinned (Romans 5:12).

Scriptural Enlightenment

Adam was the first man created by God and he had God's nature. When he disobeyed God in the Garden of Eden, he missed the mark; he sinned. As a result, he lost God's nature and received the nature of sin. Therefore, everyone born after him had his nature: the sin nature. Sin led to spiritual death, and death passed from Adam to all humankind through his bloodline. Jesus was the only one who could pay the price for the sin of humankind. Jesus paid the price with His life and blood to position humankind for peace and oneness with God again.

- ▶ Adam's disobedience to God caused humankind to fall into sin. [A choice]
- ▶ Sin caused humankind to be separated from God with a sentence of spiritual death.
- ▶ Humankind would now be dominated by Satan with hell as their future home.

The Rescue

For God so loved the world, that he gave his only begotten Son, that whosoever believeth in him should not perish, but have everlasting life (John 3:16).

[Reveal in a way they cannot deny]

Scriptural Enlightenment

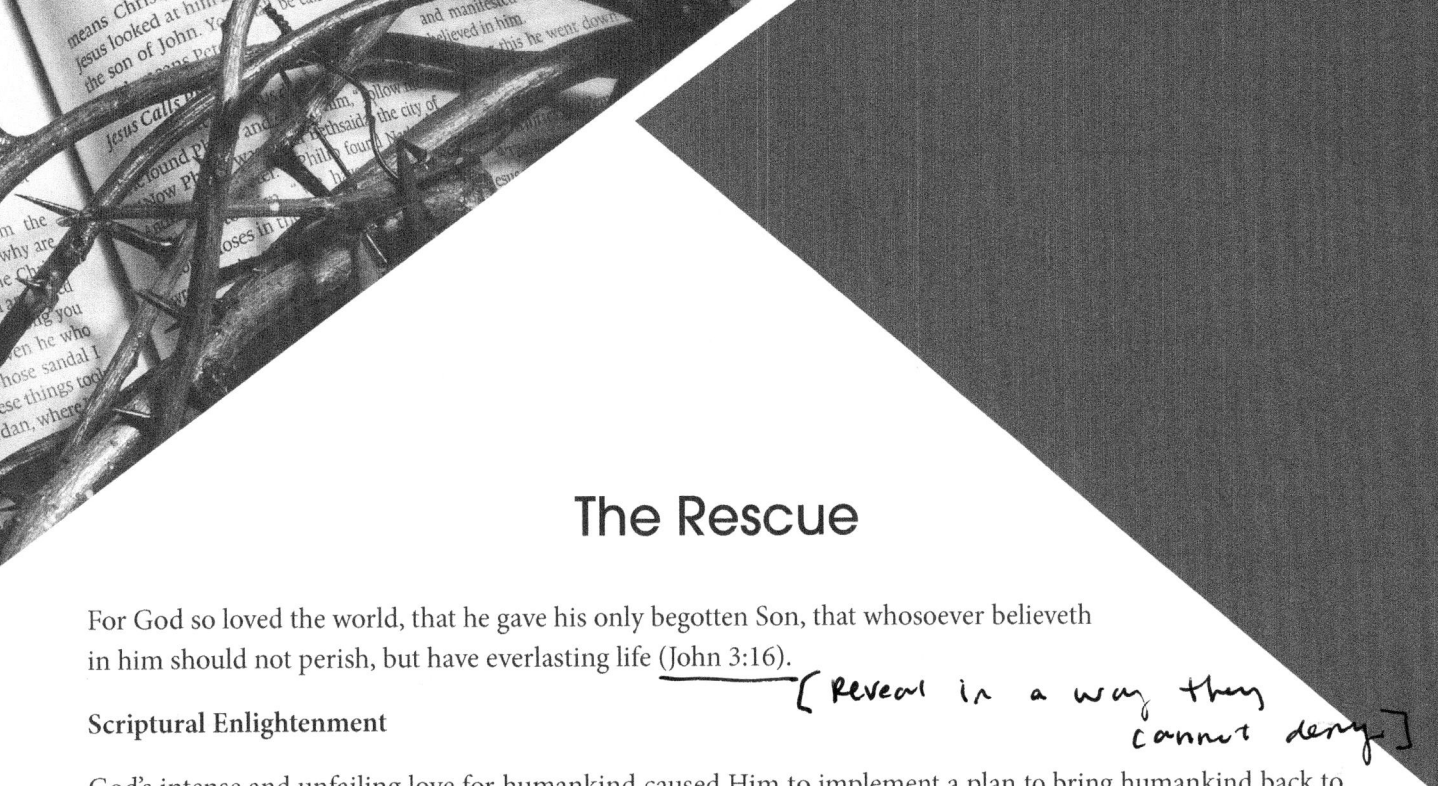

God's intense and unfailing love for humankind caused Him to implement a plan to bring humankind back to Himself. His plan cost Him His only Son, Jesus. His Son was without sin, but through obedience to God, He became sin, so that humans might receive a new nature: the nature of God. With a new nature, humankind does not have to die but can receive everlasting life. Humankind must believe upon God's Son, Jesus Christ. In doing so, they will not perish or die spiritually; but they shall receive salvation and live eternally with Him.

- ▶ God is the creator of humankind.
- ▶ God determined that humankind was worthy of saving.
- ▶ All of humankind was originally to be a part of God's family.
- ▶ From God's perspective, due to the gift of Jesus given, humankind should not perish or die spiritually.
- ▶ Receiving or rejecting Jesus Christ as Lord and Savior is a decision that every person must make.

[ALWAYS suposed to be in the family]

The Savior

Neither is there salvation in any other: for there is none other name under heaven given among men, whereby we must be saved (Acts 4:12).

Scriptural Enlightenment

Because Jesus is the sinless sacrifice who paid the price for humankind's sin, His name is the only name by which mankind can be saved. When someone is saved, they are rescued from the life that Satan had planned for them, and they receive the gift of salvation.

- ▶ Salvation includes more than Jesus' rescuing humankind from sin. It also includes safety, health, prosperity, and preservation.
- ▶ No man or spirit can grant humankind the gift of salvation.

The New You

But what saith it? The word is nigh thee, even in thy mouth, and in thy heart: that is, the word of faith, which we preach; That if thou shalt confess with thy mouth the Lord Jesus, and shalt believe in thine heart that God hath raised him from the dead, thou shalt be saved. For with the heart man believeth unto righteousness; and with the mouth confession is made unto salvation. ...For whosoever shall call upon the name of the Lord shall be saved (Romans 10:8-10, 13).

Scriptural Enlightenment

When someone acknowledges with their mouth that Jesus is the only Lord and believes in their heart that God has raised Jesus from the dead, they receive the salvation purchased by Jesus. The very moment that person accepts Jesus in their heart, they are rescued from sin and its effect, and from Satan and his dominion.

Believers obtain all the benefits of being saved and rescued from sin: safety, health, prosperity, and preservation for the total person.

All of this happens through an exchange. Jesus took our sin, and we took His righteousness or right standing with God. God no longer sees us in sin; He sees us cleansed by the shed blood of His Son.

Wow! That's a lot to receive, and all we must do is believe it and take it!

- ▶ Mankind's salvation is as near as man's mouth and heart.
- ▶ Belief in Jesus and the profession of Jesus as Lord is necessary to receive salvation.
- ▶ Rescue, safety, health, prosperity, and preservation are obtained through salvation.
- ▶ Jesus takes our sins, and He gives us His righteousness.

The Gift

For by grace are ye saved through faith; and that not of yourselves: it is the gift of God: Not of works, lest any man should boast (Ephesians 2:8-9).

Scriptural Enlightenment

God's grace provided Jesus as a gift to humankind. Salvation cannot be earned or bought. God chose to give salvation to humankind freely, but faith must be activated to take God's provision.

- ▶ Jesus is God's present to humankind.
- ▶ God's greatest gift to humankind requires no work from man.

The Adoption

But as many as received him, to them gave he power to become sons of God, even to them that believe on his name (John 1:12).

Scriptural Enlightenment

When humans receive Jesus as Lord and Savior, they receive the privilege and authority to become children of God. They can partake of the full benefit of being members of God's family.

▶ Humans receive a new family when they choose Jesus as Lord and Savior. [Family, Love, acceptance]

▶ If someone chooses and professes Jesus as Lord and Savior, they become a child of God.

> *"I am under the impression that it is not that people don't want to receive Jesus, but that they just don't know enough about Him!"*
>
> —Evangelist Marie Diggs

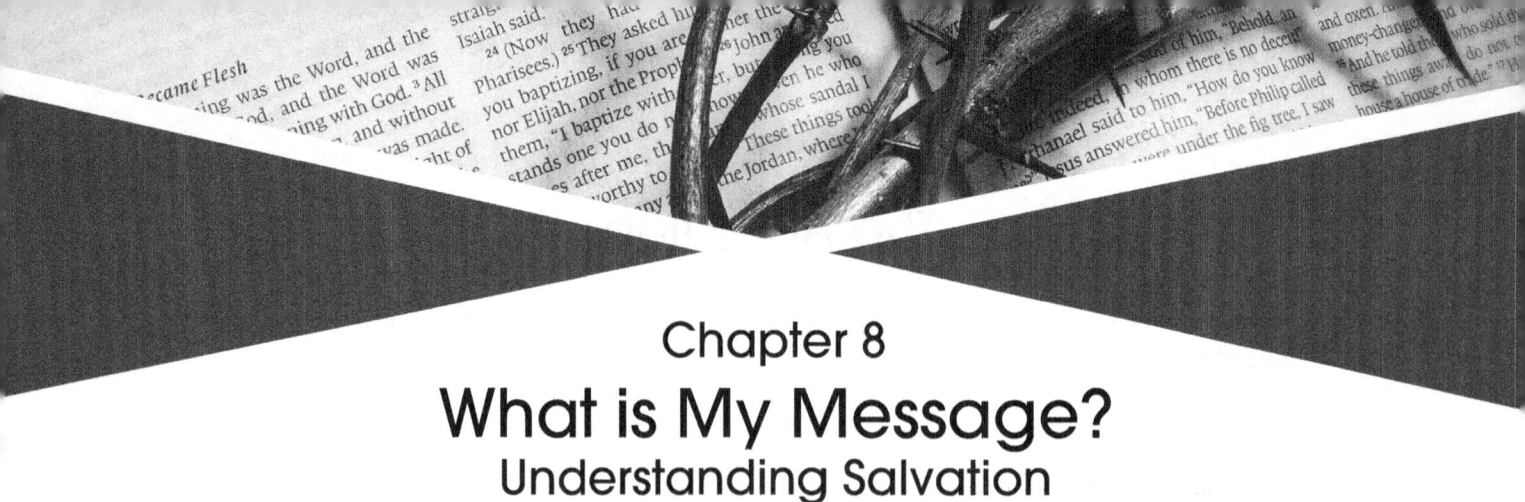

Chapter 8
What is My Message?
Understanding Salvation

1. In John 1:12, when humans get saved, they become members of _____ family.

2. "Missed the mark" is another phrase for _____, which is what Adam did when he disobeyed God.

3. Sin led to _____, and death passed from Adam to all humankind through his bloodline.

4. Adam was the first man created by God, and he had God's _____.

5. Jesus was the only one who could pay the price for humankind's sin with His _____ and _____.

6. When did God so love the world?

7. When Adam disobeyed God, he lost God's nature and received the nature of _____.

8. Through Jesus' shed blood, He positioned humankind to be at peace and _____ with God again.

9. What is the exchange that takes place when humankind receives Jesus as Savior?

10. In Ephesians 2:8-9, salvation is a _____.

887
him to Jesus.
"You are Simon
be called Cephas
means Christ).
Jesus looked at him
the son of John.
and manifested his
believed in him.
this he went down
Jesus Calls
the city of
the wilderness,'
Lord,' as the
been
sked him
you are
26 John
Proph
with
whose sandal I
do n
These things took
the Jordan, where
Behold, an
whom there is no deceit!"
Nathanael said to him, "How do you know
Jesus answered him, "Before Philip called
you, when you were under the fig tree, I saw
you." 49 Nathanael answered him, "Rabbi, you
are the Son of God! You are the King of Israel!"
50 Jesus answered him, "Because I said to you,
'I saw you under the fig tree,' do you believe?
You will see greater things than these." 51 And
he said to him, "Truly, truly, I say to you,
will see heaven opened, and the angels of G
ascending and descending on the Son of M
The Wedding at Cana
2 On the third day there was a we
Cana in Galilee, and the mothe
was there. 2 Jesus also was invited
ding with his disciples. 3 When the
mother of Jesus said to him,
Jesus said to her
them all out
and oxen.
money-cha
16 And he
these
house
was before
the witness:
John
like a
I myself did
me to baptize
whom you see
this is he who
34 And I have

Chapter 9
Salvation Scriptures and Prayer for Evangelizing

In this chapter, you'll find a list of the Scriptures featured in Chapter 8. Meditate on each Scripture and begin to commit them to memory. As you memorize them, they will flow from your spirit with ease while evangelizing.

Goal

Use the one-month calendar (make a copy using the template on page vi) to help you chart your progress. Continue to meditate on the Scriptures even after you have committed them to memory.

The Sin Issue – Romans 5:12
Wherefore, as by one man sin entered into the world, and death by sin; and so death passed upon all men, for that all have sinned.

The Rescue – John 3:16
For God so loved the world, that he gave his only begotten Son, that whosoever believeth in him should not perish, but have everlasting life.

The Savior – Acts 4:12
Neither is there salvation in any other: for there is none other name under heaven given among men, whereby we must be saved.

The New You – Romans 10:8-10, 13
But what saith it? The word is nigh thee, even in thy mouth, and in thy heart: that is, the word of faith, which we preach: That if thou shalt confess with thy mouth the Lord Jesus, and shalt believe in thine heart that God hath raised him from the dead, thou shalt be saved. For with the heart man believeth unto righteousness; and with the mouth confession is made unto salvation. ...For whosoever shall call upon the name of the Lord shall be saved.

The Gift – Ephesians 2:8-9
For by grace are ye saved through faith; and that not of yourselves: it is the gift of God: Not of works, lest any man should boast.

The Adoption – John 1:12
But as many as received him, to them gave he power to become sons of God, even to them that believe on his name.

Salvation Prayer

Below is a prayer of salvation that you can use to lead someone into receiving Christ in their heart. Simply ask the person to repeat the prayer of salvation after you.

Dear Father,

I believe that you sent your Son Jesus to die on the cross for my sins.
I believe that Jesus is no longer dead, but He has risen and is alive!
Jesus, I ask you to come into my heart now and save me.
I believe with my heart, and I confess with my mouth that you,
Jesus, are my Lord and Savior.

In your name I pray, Amen.

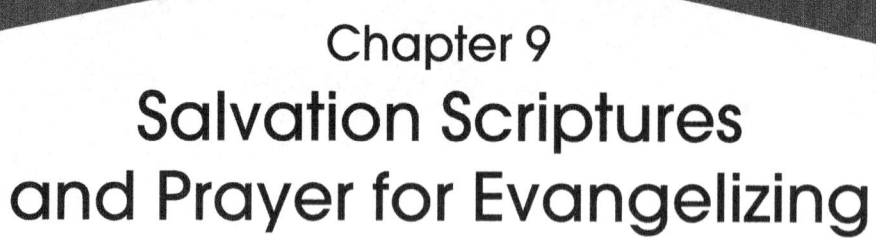

Chapter 9
Salvation Scriptures and Prayer for Evangelizing

1. According to Romans 10:8-10, 13, what two things must be done to receive biblical salvation?

2. According to John 3:16, why did God give His Son, Jesus?

3. According to Acts 4:12, why is Jesus the only man by which salvation can be received?

4. According to Ephesians 2:8-9, why can't you do good works to be saved?

5. According to Romans 5:12, explain why humans need a Savior.

6. Practice praying and leading someone through the Salvation Prayer.

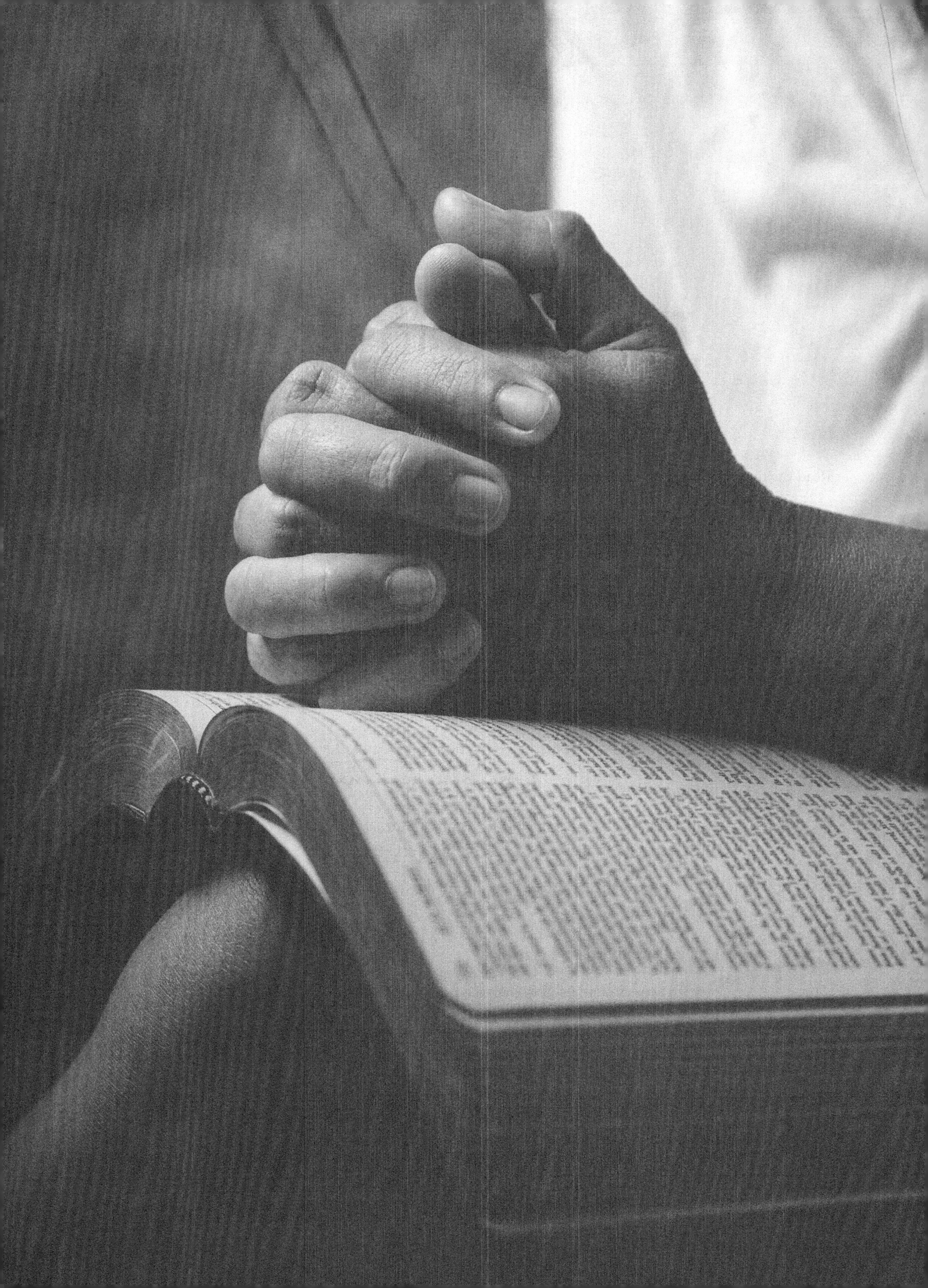

Chapter 10
Tips for Witnessing to the Unsaved

Read the tips below and begin to incorporate them into your witnessing opportunities.

✔	Check the tips that help you the most.

Realize that the person you witness to may know nothing about God's Word.

Do not communicate beyond the person's level of understanding; keep it simple.

Do not have an attitude of superiority because you are saved and they are not.

Always exude confidence in Jesus and in God's Word.

Do not argue or debate with the person.

Listen to the person as their conversation will identify their spiritual condition.

Remain on the subject. [Ask him to come into your heart]

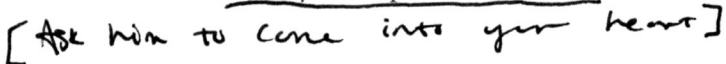

Remember that the person is blinded and cannot see properly according to 2 Corinthians 4:3-4. They do not know that there is a better life. Help them see it!

Share the benefits of salvation and how it would apply to them should they receive Jesus as Savior.

Compel them to receive Jesus.

Help the person understand that salvation is a gift that they cannot work to obtain.

Assist the person in understanding that because they have a sin nature, they do not have a choice to determine whether they will sin. Rather, they are a slave to sin due to their current nature.

Encourage the person with God's Word and bring hope to them for a better life on this Earth and in eternity.

Explain to the person that Jesus will save them no matter how far away they are from Him. No past or present sins are greater than His love for them.

✓ Check the tips that help you the most.

Pay close attention to the person's body language, as it will express the person's agreement or disagreement. It will also convey if the person is comfortable or uncomfortable with you.

Explain to the person that they will receive a new spirit according to 2 Corinthians 5:17-18.

Clarify for the person that changes in their thought life and behavior will happen when their mind is changed or renewed to God's Word, according to Romans 12:1-2.

After a person receives salvation, leave them with material to further their growth in Christ, be it a Bible, your church information, and/or the Marie Diggs Ministries Be Bold app.

Should it be appropriate, exchange information with the person to follow up on their growth in Christ. Invite them to your church, to your church's events, and/or to fellowship with other believers.

If appropriate, check on them on occasion, letting them know that you care.

If the person does not receive salvation, if appropriate, occasionally invite them to your church, to your church's events, and/or to fellowship with other believers. However, use wisdom on the amount of time spent with the person as they should not be your best friend according to 2 Corinthians 6:14-18.

Should the person not receive salvation, never give up on them. Be the voice echoing God's love, forgiveness, and restoration.

Cover them in constant prayer and speak the Word of God over them.

How will your witnessing approach change based upon the tips selected?

Journal how people responded to you based upon your new approach.

Chapter 10
Tips for Witnessing to the Unsaved

1. The believer should always help the person understand that salvation is a _____ and they can't _____ to obtain it.

2. Listening to a person's conversation will identify their what?

3. Paying attention to a person's body language will indicate a person's _____ or _____.

4. If a person does not receive salvation before the conversation ends, what should the believer do?

5. What is a key thing to realize when witnessing to a person?

6. When witnessing, help the person to understand that because of their sin nature they are _____.

7. If a person chooses not to receive salvation, what should the believer do?

8. When ministering to a person the believer should always do what?

Chapter 11
What Is My Message?
Understanding Rededication

Read every Scripture and the scriptural enlightenments. Meditate on God's messages in each passage. You'll find all the Scriptures from this chapter printed without commentary in the next chapter. That list will be a helpful tool for meditation and memorization.

1 John 1:9
If we confess our sins, he is faithful and just to forgive us our sins, and to cleanse us from all unrighteousness.

1 John 2:1-2
My little children, these things write I unto you, that ye sin not. And if any man sin, we have an advocate with the Father, Jesus Christ the righteous: And he is the propitiation for our sins: and not for ours only, but also for the sins of the whole world.

Scriptural Enlightenment

▶ God is not a man; He keeps His promises. You can trust Him to make you clean again.

▶ No stain of sin is greater than the power of Jesus' blood that cleanses us from all sin.

▶ When you confess and acknowledge your sins before the Father, Jesus becomes your advocate or intercessor, intervening on your behalf to the Father.

▶ Jesus is the propitiation, atonement, or expiation for our sins. The sacrifice of His life freed us from the penalty of our sins.

▶ Confess your sins immediately, repent, and turn from them asking for strength to stay free of them.

▶ Daily meditation of Scriptures on the topic of a weakness builds a solid faith foundation and in time will keep you from falling in that area of your life.

The Prodigal Son

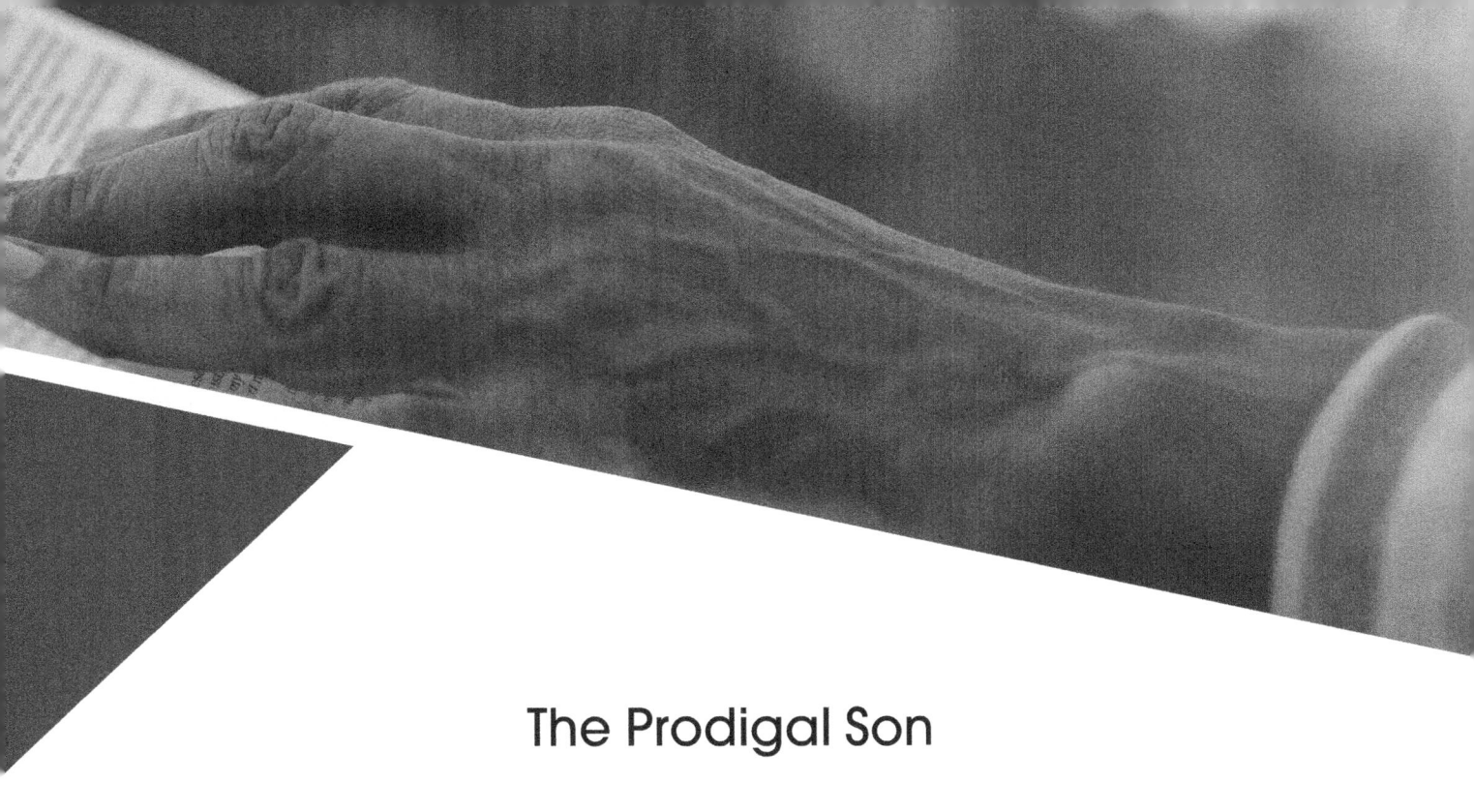

To see God's unfailing love for His children when they are out of fellowship, read the account of the prodigal son in Luke 15:11-32. Then answer the following questions:

1. What does "riotous living" mean (v. 13)? Use a good Bible concordance to answer this question.

2. When did things start to go bad for the prodigal son?

3. When did he have a change of attitude?

4. When did he have a change of heart?

5. In verses 21 and 22 note that the father did not acknowledge his son's shame and feelings of unworthiness. How did the father respond to the son's actions of repentance?

6. Use a good Bible concordance to determine what the three gifts given to the son represent.

7. Read verse 30 and write down how the prodigal son's actions towards his brother mimic too many believers who are aware of other believers who are caught up in sin.

8. Write down a time when you were out of fellowship or backslidden and God's love actively came after you.

9. Write down how you felt when you realized that God still loved you and accepted you regardless of your mistakes and wrongdoings.

10. How did God's love change the way that you saw Him and interacted with Him?

> *"As Christians, we should fervently go after our backslidden and out-of-fellowship brothers and sisters instead of leaving them hurt on the battlefield."*
> —Evangelist Marie Diggs

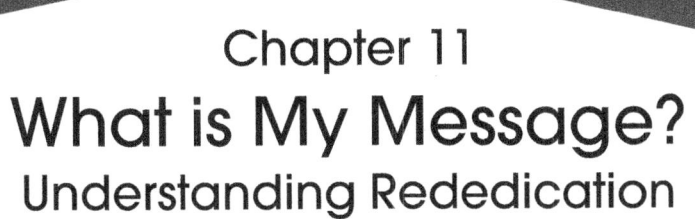

Chapter 11
What is My Message?
Understanding Rededication

1. No stain of sin is greater than what?

2. The sacrifice of Jesus freed us from   .

3. When a person confesses or acknowledges their sins before the Father, Jesus becomes their what?

4. First John 2:2 says, "And he is the propitiation for our sins: and not for ours only, but also for the sins of the whole world." What does the word *propitiation* mean in this context?

5. What does daily meditation of Scriptures on the topic of a weakness build?

6. God keeps His promises; therefore, you can   Him to make you   again.

Chapter 12
Rededication Scriptures and Prayer for Evangelizing

In this chapter, you'll find a list of the Scriptures featured in Chapter 11. Meditate on each Scripture and begin to commit them to memory. As you memorize them, they will flow from your spirit with ease while evangelizing.

Goal

Use the one-month calendar (make a copy using the template on page vi) to help you chart your progress. Continue to meditate on the Scriptures even after you have committed them to memory.

1 John 1:9
If we confess our sins, he is faithful and just to forgive us our sins, and to cleanse us from all unrighteousness.

1 John 2:1-2
My little children, these things write I unto you, that ye sin not. And if any man sin, we have an advocate with the Father, Jesus Christ the righteous: 2 And he is the propitiation for our sins: and not for ours only, but also for the sins of the whole world.

Rededication Prayer

Below is a prayer of rededication that you can use to lead someone back into fellowship with God. Ask the person to repeat the prayer after you and to confess their sins to God underneath their breath asking for forgiveness.

Dear Father,

In the name of Jesus, I confess and acknowledge my sins before you. I ask you to forgive me and to cleanse me from all unrighteousness. Because you are faithful and just, I know that my sins are forgiven and that I am in right standing with you. I am free from past sins.

In His name, I pray, Amen.

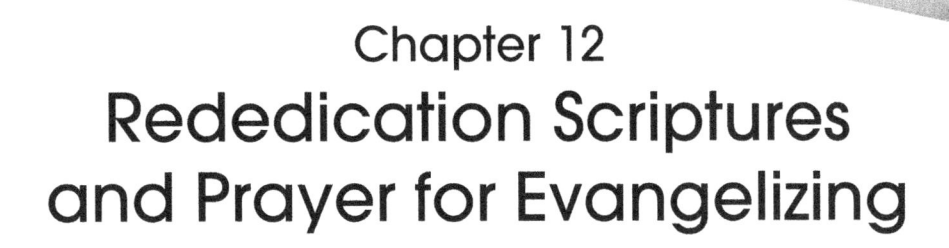

Chapter 12
Rededication Scriptures and Prayer for Evangelizing

1. When a person confesses or acknowledges their sins before the Father, Jesus becomes their what?

2. What Scripture documents that we have a forgiving God who loves us?

3. Who is our advocate with the Father and has the power to forgive us our sins?

4. Practice praying and leading someone through the Rededication Prayer.

Chapter 13
Tips for Witnessing to those Out-of-Fellowship & Backslidden

Read the witnessing tips below and begin to incorporate them into your witnessing opportunities.

✔	Check the tips that help you the most.
	Realize that a believer's relationship with God is not broken when they are out of fellowship with God or backslidden. Rather, their fellowship with God has been broken due to sin.
	Encourage the believer to immediately acknowledge and confess their sins to God.
	Always exude confidence in Jesus and in God's Word.
	Help the believer to understand that they do not have to wait until they get to a church service to get things right with God. Acknowledgment, confession, and forgiveness of sins can transpire when sins are committed.
	Explain to the believer that God has not "left them" due to sins committed as referenced in Hebrews 13:5.
	Encourage the believer not to allow the feelings of shame, guilt, and embarrassment to keep them from God and church attendance.
	Help the believer to comprehend that no sin is greater than the blood of Jesus to cleanse, forgive, and restore!
	Do not isolate the believer; however, use wisdom regarding how much time you spend with them.
	Do not force the believer to get things right with God. Allow God to work on their heart.

✔ Check the tips that help you the most.

Remember, out-of-fellowship and backslidden believers are unfulfilled, unhappy, irritated, and convicted by the Holy Ghost. Do not be fooled by their seemingly happy lifestyle.

Should it be appropriate, exchange information with the person to follow up on their growth in Christ and to invite them to your church, to your church's events, and/or to fellowship with other believers.

If appropriate, check up on them on occasion, letting them know that you care.

If the person does not receive rededication when you witness to them, if appropriate, occasionally invite them to your church, to your church's events, or to fellowship with other believers. However, use wisdom on the amount of time spent with the person as they should not be your best friend according to 2 Corinthians 6:14-18.

Keep the door of communication open.

Never give up on them; be the voice echoing God's love, forgiveness, and restoration.

Constantly cover them in prayer and speak the Word of God over them.

After a person receives rededication, leave them material to further their growth in Christ, be it a Bible, your church information, and/or, the Marie Diggs Ministries Be Bold app.

How will your witnessing approach change based upon the tips selected?

Journal how people responded to you based upon your new approach.

Goal

Make a list of people who are out-of-fellowship with God or are backslidden. Take two weeks and purposefully decide to pray aloud Ephesians 1:16-21 over them adding their names to the Scriptures.

1.

2.

3.

At the end of the two weeks, as you are led by God's Spirit, call the people on the list or go to see them, and minister rededication to them. Use the one-month calendar (make a copy using the template on page vi) to help you chart who decides to rededicate themselves to God. Give God glory for every brother or sister in Christ who decides to return to God and receives His forgiveness.

Chapter 13
Tips for Witnessing to Out-of-Fellowship and Backslidden Believers

1. How should the believer encourage the backslidden believer?

2. Sin breaks the _____ with God, not the _____.

3. When witnessing to out-of-fellowship/backslidden believers, do not be fooled by their what?

Supernatural Help

In this Section:

▶ **Evangelism Is About Partnership**
When believers work together in harmony with their supernatural partners, evangelizing can truly be successful!

▶ **Understanding Your Supernatural Equipment**
Evangelism is a supernatural assignment; therefore, supernatural tools are needed to accomplish its tasks.

Chapter 14
Evangelism Is About Partnership

Partnership is working together with others to carry out a task. God never designed believers to evangelize without supernatural partners. When believers work together in harmony with their partners, evangelizing can truly be successful!

Read the Scripture references in each point and describe how each of the partners helps you when you evangelize.

Partners in Evangelism

- ▶ **The Father God** – Hebrews 2:4
- ▶ **Jesus** – Mark 16:15-20
- ▶ **Holy Spirit** - Acts 16:6-10, John 16:13
- ▶ **Angels** – Hebrews 1:14, Psalm 103:20

Believers can boldly evangelize when they realize that they are not alone. When they follow Jesus' example of teaching and preaching, they get the opportunity to work with the Godhead and to experience the supernatural. Wow, what a privilege!

Jesus taught His disciples how to witness. As you obey His Word about sharing the Gospel, He will teach you how to witness through the Holy Ghost.

When you read Mark 1:16-17 you will find that Jesus trained His disciples to catch men instead of fish. Using a good Bible concordance, define the word *become* in verse 17.

Mark 1:16-17
Now as he walked by the sea of Galilee, he saw Simon and Andrew his brother casting a net into the sea: for they were fishers. And Jesus said unto them, Come ye after me, and I will make you to become fishers of men.

Write down the steps that you believe would be necessary for you to become a "fisher of men."

Jesus didn't preach, teach, or heal without help. The Father and the Holy Spirit were with Him.

Read Acts 10:38 and jot down the three persons of the Trinity involved in ministry to people. Take a moment and look up the word *power* in a good Bible concordance and in the space below write down its definition.

1.

2.

3.

Acts 10:38
How God anointed Jesus of Nazareth with the Holy Ghost and with power: who went about doing good, and healing all that were oppressed of the devil; for God was with him.

"With heaven guiding our steps, we are sure to bankrupt hell!"
—Evangelist Marie Diggs

Chapter 14
Evangelism is About Partnership

1. Who are a believer's supernatural partners?

   a.

   b.

   c.

   d.

2. What is the definition of *partnership*?

3. Jesus did not preach, teach, or heal without help. Who was with Him?

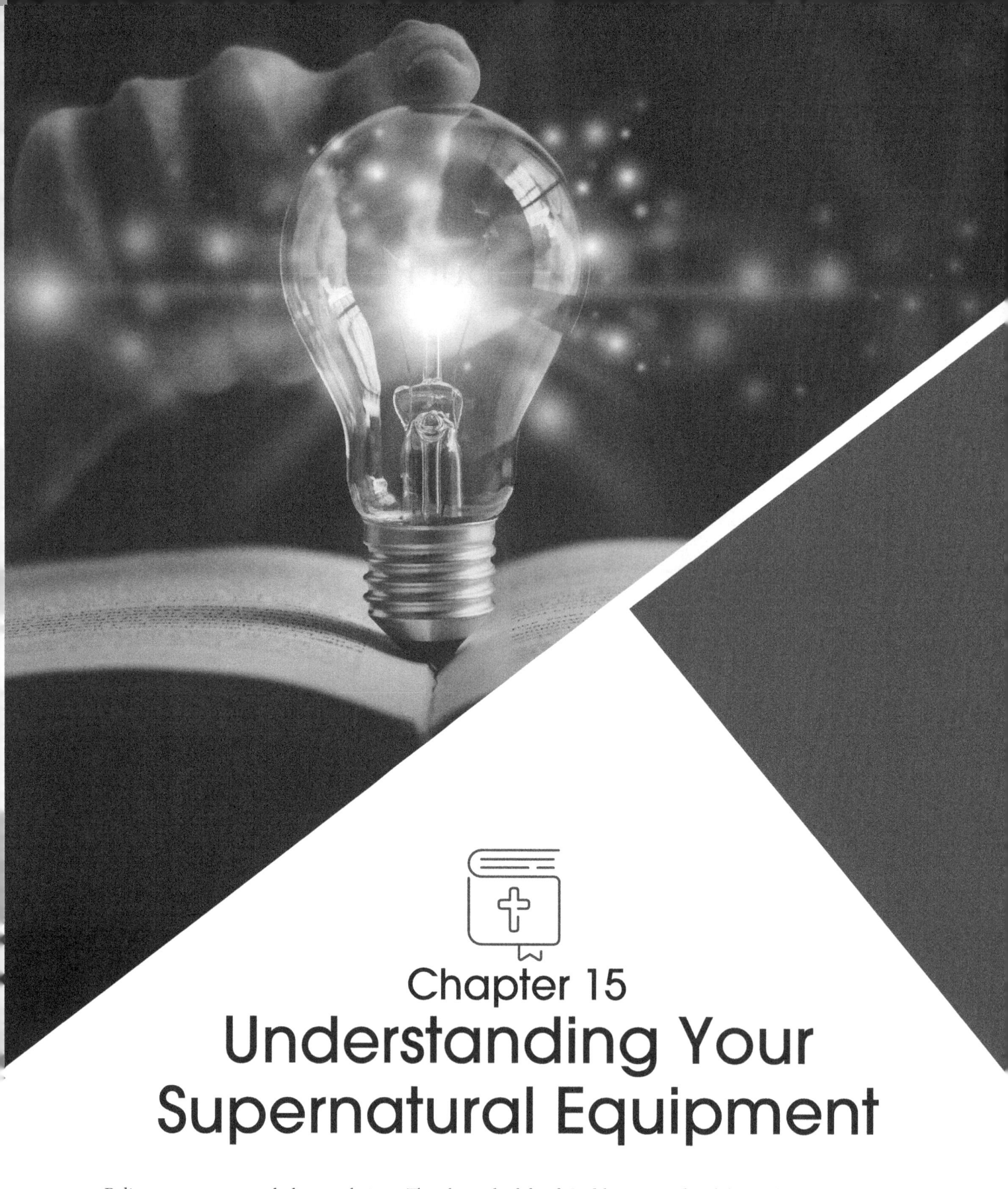

Chapter 15
Understanding Your Supernatural Equipment

Believers are not merely human beings. They have the life of God living inside of them, that is, in their spirit. They have been positioned by God to live a supernatural life empowered by His Spirit and by His living Word. Evangelism is a supernatural assignment; therefore, supernatural tools are needed to accomplish its tasks. Jesus transferred His power and authority, and God gave His Spirit to the body of Christ to empower them on the Earth to continue Jesus' work.

Believers' Empowerment Equipment for Evangelism

▶ **Delegated and Transferred Authority**
Read Matthew 28:18-20 and use a good Bible concordance to define the word *power* in verse 18 and the words *Go ye* in verse 19. Now describe in your own words what this means for you as a believer.

▶ **The Powerful Name of Jesus**
In Mark 16:15-20 Jesus gives a command to the body of Christ. Read this portion of Scripture and write down who will be unable to work should believers not do their part in evangelizing. Also, define the word *name* in verse 17 using a good Bible concordance. Write down its definition and how it plays a part in your sharing Christ with others.

▶ **A Powerful Promise**
Whenever Jesus gives someone a gift, I believe that the gift is important and needful. Read Luke 24:46-49 and write down how needful you think it is for you to receive the promise.

▶ **Empowered to Evangelize**
Read Acts 1:8 and write down when the power is received. Also, write down when the disciples were to become witnesses of Jesus. Lastly, define the word *power* in this verse of Scripture in a good Bible concordance and write down its meaning.

▶ **Powerful Manifestations of the Holy Spirit**
First Corinthians 12:7-11 lists the gifts of the Spirit, which can operate through a believer's witnessing to others should the Spirit of God determine to use a believer in that way. List the nine gifts of the Spirit and use a good Bible concordance to define each spiritual gift. Write down the experience you had when one of the gifts of the Spirit was in operation through you.

▶ **God's Unchanging and Enduring Word**
Read 1 Peter 1:23-25 and think about how awesome it is to have the privilege to share God's Word that is imperishable and immortal.

▶ **God's Powerful Word**
When ministering God's Word, it is a joy to know that His Word is working on the hearts of the people with whom you are speaking. Read Hebrews 4:12-13 and write down what it means to you to have the living Word of God actively at work while you minister.

Chapter 15
Understanding Your Supernatural Equipment

1. List the seven parts of the Believers' Empowerment Equipment for Evangelism:

   a.

   b.

   c.

   d.

   e.

   f.

   g.

2. Why are believers not merely human beings?

3. Why do believers need supernatural tools to accomplish the task of soul-winning?

4. What was transferred by God and Jesus to empower believers to continue Jesus' work on the Earth?

5. How have believers been positioned by God to live a supernatural life?

The Practical Side of Evangelism

In this Section:

▶ Systematic Method for Presenting the Gospel
Evangelism is the spreading of the good news of the Gospel of Jesus Christ.

▶ How to Begin Evangelizing
It is simply beginning a conversation with someone, listening to them, and when the time is right, interjecting what God has provided for them through Jesus Christ.

▶ Your Personal Testimony: A Powerful Tool
Your life's story paints a picture of God's love in action and Jesus' sacrifice.

Chapter 16
Systematic Method for Presenting the Gospel

In this chapter, you'll find nine easy steps that will help you in your approach from start to finish when beginning to witness.

Step One
Identify to whom you will evangelize.

For each point write down the names of people who come to mind. (Keep in mind that a "new connection" is a stranger because you did not know them prior to addressing them with the Gospel presentation.)

▶ New Connection

▶ Co-Worker

▶ Acquaintance

▶ Friend

▶ Family Member

Step Two
Identify the best approach to begin evangelizing.

The best approach to begin evangelizing is to ensure that you have the proper training to skillfully minister to people. This includes the following:

▶ Complete this Answer the Call Be Bold Evangelism Workbook

▶ Gain experience through witnessing

▶ Watch people who are experienced in sharing Christ

▶ Observe and target whom you should approach with the Gospel

Have some of the noted points been a help to you in the past? If so, write down how they've helped you.

Step Three
Identify the spiritual condition of the person.

In my experiences, generally, listening intently and asking key questions assist me in determining a person's spiritual condition.

Write down how listening intently and asking key questions could possibly benefit your witnessing experience. A key question could be, "Have you ever asked Jesus to come into your heart?" or "Do you want to be free from that situation?"

Step Four
Inform the person of what Jesus has provided for their specific situation.

These may include:

- ▶ Healing
- ▶ Peace
- ▶ Supernatural Provision
- ▶ Restoration
- ▶ Protection
- ▶ Salvation or Rededication

Write down two Scriptures of God's promise for each point.

Healing	

Peace	

Step Five:
Utilize your personal testimony when it is relevant.

Write down when your personal testimony led someone to want to receive salvation or rededication.

Step Six
Share the benefits of receiving Jesus as Lord and Savior.

Below are some benefits to receiving Jesus as Lord and Savior.

- Rescue and deliverance from sin, spiritual death, Satan, and hell
- Receiving a new family, where God is your Father and Jesus is your brother
- Receiving a new nature by the Holy Spirit's indwelling you
- Having the opportunity to follow the leading and guidance of the Holy Spirit for a victorious life on Earth
- Healing, health, and wholeness for your body and mind
- Supernatural protection and preservation
- The right to use the name of Jesus
- The privilege to plead the blood of Jesus
- Angels to minister for you and on your behalf
- Receiving the nine fruits of the Spirit (Galatians 5:22-23)
- Peace in knowing that heaven is your home as you live in right standing with God

Write down how these benefits have impacted your life.

Step Seven
Lead them in the prayer that meets their spiritual condition.

Go over the prayers of salvation and rededication found on pages 41 and 52 to implant them deeper into your heart.

Step Eight
Leave them with information to assist with their growth in Christ.

▶ Salvation or rededication Scriptures

▶ Bible

▶ The Marie Diggs Ministries Be Bold app is a helpful aid for the newly saved or those coming back into fellowship with God.

Step Nine
Should it be appropriate, follow up with them and encourage their church or Bible study attendance and offer to pray with them.

▶ If the person is of the opposite sex, married, or underage, it might not be appropriate for you to follow up with them (for those who are underage, seeking parental or guardian approval for continued contact might be most appropriate).

Write down why you should have certain boundaries while ministering.

Chapter 16
Systematic Method for Presenting the Gospel

1. How do you identify the person's spiritual condition?

2. After witnessing to a person, what should you do before departing from them?

3. How should believers identify to whom they will witness?

4. List six benefits of receiving Jesus as Lord and Savior.

   a.

   b.

   c.

   d.

   e.

   f.

Chapter 17
How to Begin Evangelizing

Evangelizing is easy! It is simply beginning a conversation with someone, listening to them, and when the time is right (be it that day or weeks or months later), interjecting what God has provided for them through Jesus Christ.

People spend most of their time Monday through Friday in four places:

- ▶ At work
- ▶ At school
- ▶ At a gym/working out
- ▶ Running errands, shopping, eating out, or keeping appointments

As a result, these settings are where most believers' witnessing should transpire.

How to Begin Evangelizing? Co-workers

Write down the names of co-workers with whom you have identified to share Christ.

Name:

Name:

Name:

What Should Be My Approach?
From years of experience some of my best approaches for ministering to co-workers have been the following:

- Be yourself.

- Do not change to fit in, rather stand out.

- Don't isolate yourself from non-believing co-workers.

- Prior to engaging in witnessing, build a rapport with a co-worker, which gives you the time to identify the person's spiritual condition.

- Walk in love with co-workers.

- Do not tell co-workers what to do with their lives or situations.

- When they begin to open up and ask you for your opinions on matters, give them God's Word on the subject and then listen and pray for them.

- Follow up by asking them how things turned out.

- When the time is right, offer them salvation or rededication based on their spiritual need.

Write down the ways that you think my experiences could be helpful to you.

An Acquaintance

Write down the names of acquaintances with whom you have identified to share Christ.

Name:

Name:

Name:

What Should Be My Approach?
From years of experience some of my best approaches for ministering to acquaintances have been the following:

- ▶ Build a rapport, which gives you the time to identify the person's spiritual condition.

- ▶ Allow the person time to become comfortable with you and to determine that you are a Christian.

- ▶ When the person opens up to you, do not bombard them with Scriptures; listen to them and pray for their needs.

- ▶ Answer their questions to their issues using God's Word.

- ▶ Follow up with them regarding their prayer request.

- ▶ When the time is right, offer them salvation or rededication based on their spiritual need.

Write down the ways that you think my experiences could be helpful to you.

New Connection

Make a heart decision to target strangers to share Christ with as you go about your day. Think of ways to incorporate witnessing into your everyday life. Write down your thoughts.

What Should Be My Approach?
From years of experience some of my best approaches for ministering to new connections have been the following:

▶ Approach people who visibly need healing and offer them prayer.

▶ Approach people who are visibly sad or depressed and offer them prayer.

▶ Compliment someone on an outfit to begin a conversation.

▶ Begin a conversation while on an airplane.

▶ Approach someone for prayer while they are job hunting.

▶ Begin the conversation using the conversation starters or the phrases providing "the door" (see more details in the following sections).

▶ When the time is right, offer them salvation or rededication based upon their spiritual need.

Write down the ways that you think my experiences could be helpful to you.

Read John 4:1-42 and write down what caused Jesus to be in the same place as the woman who began the conversation. What were Jesus' first words to her? Was there a gift of the Spirit in operation during His time of ministry to the woman? Lastly, write down the result of this powerful time of ministry.

In addition, most people's Friday evenings and weekends are filled with:

▶ Relaxation

▶ Enjoyment

▶ Entertainment

▶ Self-fulfillment

As a result, you will be around many strangers in various places, including:

- Movie theatres
- Plays or concerts
- Parks
- Outdoor events
- Sports games
- Malls or shopping venues
- Beauty salons or barber shops

Therefore, believers should also take advantage of witnessing while at these various places. Most of Jesus' and His disciples' conversations and witnessing opportunities were with people that they had never met before or did not know personally. Below is a list of conversation starters that will assist you in beginning an evangelistic conversation.

Examples of Conversation Starters

- Ask someone if they have seen a particular movie and if so, how it was.
- Talk about previous movies that you've seen.
- Talk about your surroundings (i.e., the updates at the movie theater).
- Discuss the playwright of the play.
- Talk about the concert and your excitement to be attending.
- Give a compliment regarding a person's clothes, jewelry, hair, boat, etc.
- Talk about different athletes at a sporting event.
- Offer a prayer for a person's need.
- Talk about the weather.
- Talk about current events.

While conversing with the person, listen and look for "the door." "The door" represents the words that you will say that provide an entryway into the conversation about Jesus and God's Word.

When the person that you are talking to begins to speak about other things like, "the economy and how it is tough to survive in times like these," or "we are living in some scary times; look at everything going on in the world," you can interject one of the phrases that will provide the entryway into a conversation about Jesus and God.

Phrases Providing "The Door"

- I know who will do that for you.
- I know what can help you.
- I know a way out.
- I know how you feel.
- There's only one way to win in this situation.
- You don't have to continue to live like this.
- You don't have to put up with that.
- I believe in the power of prayer; let me pray for you.
- God has taken care of that already.
- Do you know that Jesus has taken care of that for you?
- I'm not concerned about that; God has made a way for me, and He'll make a way for you, too.
- Jesus has already provided healing for you.
- Jesus believes in you.
- Jesus has made a way for you.
- There is divine protection for God's children. Are you His child?
- I've been rescued from what is coming to this world; how about you?
- You're so full of joy; you must be a Christian.

Other Ways to Find "The Door"

- Ask the Holy Spirit to show you what to say.
- Observe when a person is stressed or in need of healing.
- Consider prior knowledge of someone's situation.
- Ask to pray for someone.

Also, as believers, we have family members and friends in need of salvation and rededication. Thus, knowing how to begin the steps of evangelizing them is important, too!

Family Members

Write down the names of family members with whom you have identified to share Christ.

Name:

Name:

Name:

What Should Be My Approach?
From years of experience, some of my best approaches for ministering to family members have been the following:

- Pray for them to receive salvation or rededication.
- Pray that God will send skillful laborers across their paths.
- Live a Christ-like lifestyle before them.
- Do not isolate yourself from non-believing family members.
- Do not leave a damaging impression by gossiping or talking negatively about other family members.
- Do not preach to them and tell them about their bad behavior.
- When they come to you for advice or prayer, give them God's Word.
- Wait until the time is right because, generally in time, they will be ready to take your offer of salvation or rededication.
- Be prepared if family members try to get you to do some things that you did in your life prior to receiving salvation.
- Read the following Scriptures and use them to pray over your family members: Ephesians 1:16-23, 3:14-19, and Colossians 1:9-11.

Write down the ways that you think my experiences could be helpful to you.

Friends

Write down the names of friends with whom you have identified to share Christ.

Name:

Name:

Name:

What Should Be My Approach?
From years of experience some of my best approaches for ministering to friends have been the following:

- Pray for them to receive salvation or rededication.
- Pray that God will send skillful laborers across their paths.
- Live a Christ-like lifestyle before them.
- Do not isolate yourself from non-believing friends.
- Use wisdom regarding how much time is spent with non-believing friends.
- Be led by God's Word and His Spirit regarding the activities or events that you attend with friends.
- Do not damage your witness by giving in to your friends' peer pressure.
- Do not leave a damaging impression like gossiping or talking negatively about other friends.
- Do not preach to them and tell them about their bad behavior.
- When they come to you for advice or prayer, give them God's Word.
- Wait until the time is right, and then offer them salvation or rededication based upon their spiritual need.
- Read the following Scriptures and use them to pray over your friends: Ephesians 1:16-23, 3:14-19, and Colossians 1:9-11.

Write down the ways that you think my experiences could be helpful to you.

Lastly, the Gospel is meant to be preached as a lifestyle. Believers should constantly be found ministering to others through conversational and/or relational evangelism.

The Call

God has called you an ambassador for Christ and equipped you with supernatural help along with the necessary tools to accomplish His call for your life.

Below is The Call to Action Chart. Use these charts and a copy of the one-year calendar template on page vii to track your action steps to engage in The Call.

The Call to Action Charts

Check those actions you have completed.

✔ Co-Workers

Name of Co-Worker	Praying for them/ their prayer request	Building a rapport with them	Offered Salvation	Received Salvation	Offered Rededication	Received Rededication	Gave Scriptures, Bible, or the Marie Diggs Ministries Be Bold App

✔ Acquaintances

Name of Acquaintance	Praying for them/ their prayer request	Building a rapport with them	Offered Salvation	Received Salvation	Offered Rededication	Received Rededication	Gave Scriptures, Bible, or the Marie Diggs Ministries Be Bold App

✔ New Connections

Name of New Connection	Praying for them/ their prayer request	Building a rapport with them	Offered Salvation	Received Salvation	Offered Rededication	Received Rededication	Gave Scriptures, Bible, or the Marie Diggs Ministries Be Bold App

✔ Family Members

Name of Family Member	Praying for them/ their prayer request	Building a rapport with them	Offered Salvation	Received Salvation	Offered Rededication	Received Rededication	Gave Scriptures, Bible, or the Marie Diggs Ministries Be Bold App

✔ Friends

Name of Friend	Praying for them/ their prayer request	Building a rapport with them	Offered Salvation	Received Salvation	Offered Rededication	Received Rededication	Gave Scriptures, Bible, or the Marie Diggs Ministries Be Bold App

The Call to Action Chart for New Connections

✓	PLACE A CHECK BY WHAT APPLIES TO YOU.
	I am approaching people who visibly need healing.
	I am approaching people who are visibly sad or depressed.
	I am complimenting people on their attire.
	I am approaching people for prayer.
	I am beginning conversations with new connections on airplanes, at the salon, at the grocery store, etc.
	I am actively ministering to new connections.

▶ **Number of people who received salvation?**

▶ **Number of people who received rededication?**

Give God glory for every person's eternity that has been altered due to your obedience to God's Word and yielding to His call on your life!

> *"It's time-out for silent Christianity!*
> *People are waiting on you to begin a conversation with them*
> *that will change their nature and impact their eternal lives."*
>
> —Evangelist Marie Diggs

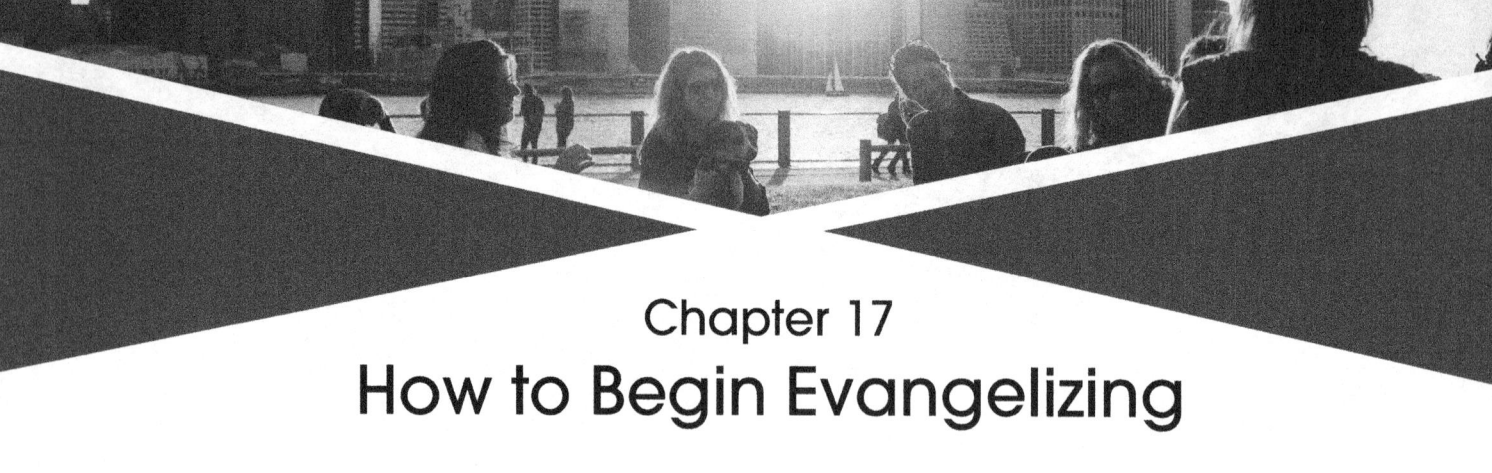

Chapter 17
How to Begin Evangelizing

1. What does "the door" represent?

2. List five phrases that you will use to assist you in entering "the door":

   a.

   b.

   c.

   d.

   e.

3. List two examples of conversations that you'll be comfortable using as a conversation starter:

   a.

   b.

4. "The door" is found in what four ways?

   a.

   b.

   c.

   d.

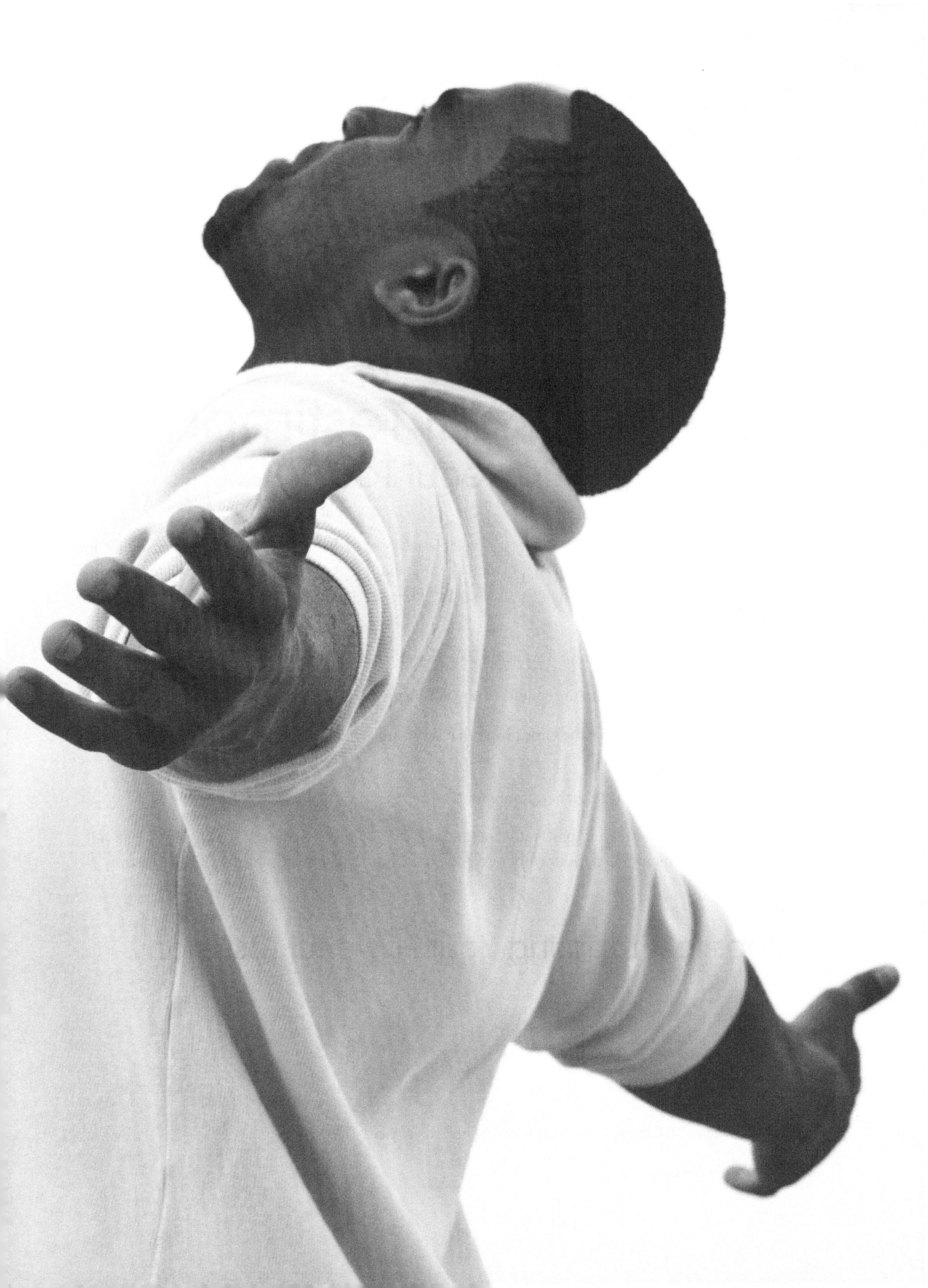

Chapter 18
Your Personal Testimony:
A Powerful Tool

Everyone is created unique by God. However, it's possible to cross paths with people who have similar life experiences from time to time. When this opportunity arises, and the person needs salvation or rededication unashamedly, share your personal testimony allowing your life's story to paint a picture of God's love in action and Jesus' sacrifice.

When sharing your personal testimony, be explicitly transparent. Transparency provides the following:

- It helps people to identify with the condition of your life prior to receiving salvation.
- It causes people to realize that the same power that saved and delivered you can and will save and deliver them, too.
- It causes the person to imagine a new future for themselves.

Therefore, do not be ashamed of your past; rather, allow your past to help free others. Confidently and boldly share your personal testimony and let your story be a powerful witnessing tool to impact someone's eternity.

Steps for Preparing Your Powerful Testimony

- Realize that you have a story to tell.
- Recognize that people need to hear your story.
- Decide to unashamedly share your story.
- Identify when to tell the story of your personal life experiences.
- Be explicitly transparent.

Write Your Powerful Testimony

Answer the following questions to help you write your testimony.

How was your life prior to receiving Jesus in your heart?

Why did you choose to receive salvation?

What has your life looked like since you've lived in fellowship with God and in His Word?

"Your testimony is someone else's lifeline."
—Evangelist Marie Diggs

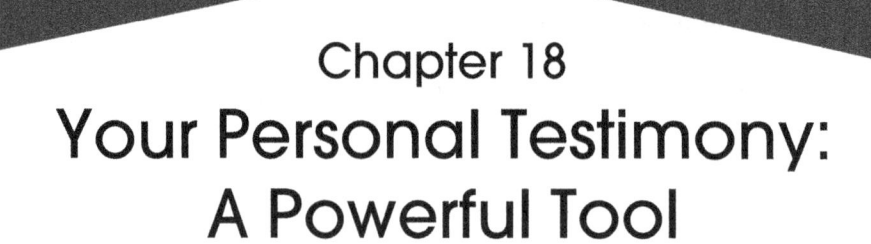

Chapter 18
Your Personal Testimony: A Powerful Tool

1. What will the power of your story do?

2. When possible, allow your life story to paint a picture of God's goodness.

3. Why is transparency so important?

4. Why should you be transparent when sharing your life story?

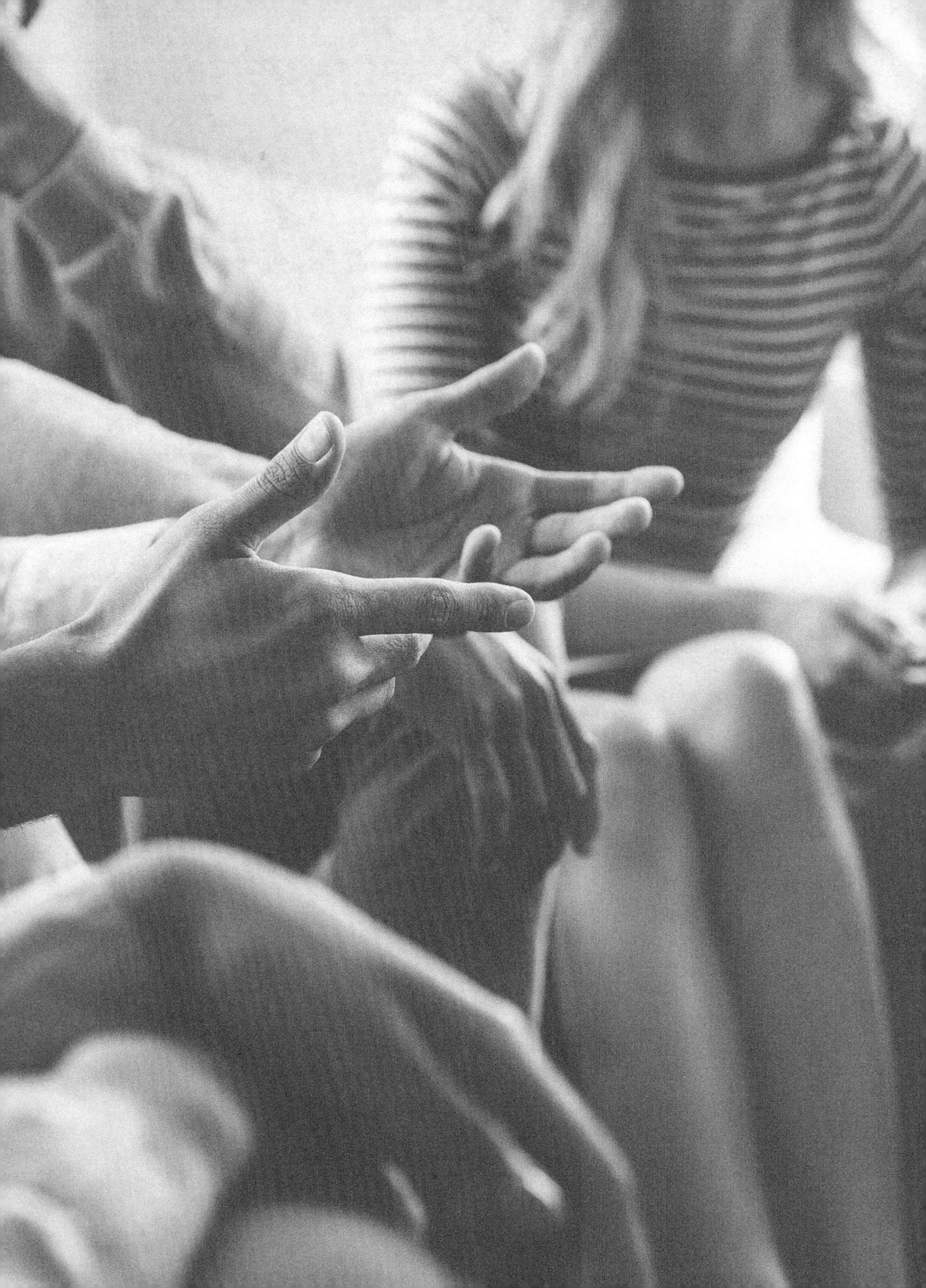

Understanding People

In this Section:

▶ **Understanding Your Audience**
If you have a good grasp of what makes people tick, you have an advantage when sharing the Gospel with others.

▶ **Ministering to the Hurting**
Unfortunately, many live a life where hurt and pain have totally overtaken them.

Chapter 19
Understanding Your Audience

To evangelize effectively, you must understand people—your audience. We all have different backgrounds and come from various places, but we all have the same needs. When you have a good grasp of what makes people tick, you have an advantage when sharing the Gospel with others.

We all need:

- ▶ To be loved
- ▶ To have family and friends (acceptance or belonging)
- ▶ To have joy or happiness
- ▶ To be healthy
- ▶ To live in safety
- ▶ To have purpose and fulfillment
- ▶ To be provided for

In addition, many people are starving for real answers to the issues that plague their lives. Also, many people feel:

- Fearful
- Hurt
- Confused
- Depressed
- Suicidal
- Hopeless
- Lost
- Unfulfilled

When believers are aware that people are experiencing one or more of these feelings in their lives, it becomes easy to share the benefits of what Jesus has done for them. People who have yet to receive Jesus as Savior are empty and unfulfilled. They are primed and ready to hear the Gospel.

Write down the Scriptures that you lean on when you are experiencing one or more of the ways many people feel. Since the Scriptures that you identified help you, they will likely help someone else who is experiencing the same feelings.

Chapter 19
Understanding Your Audience

1. When we have a good grasp of what makes people tick, what do we gain?

2. Why is it that people who have yet to receive Jesus are primed and ready to hear the Gospel?

3. To evangelize effectively, whom must we understand?

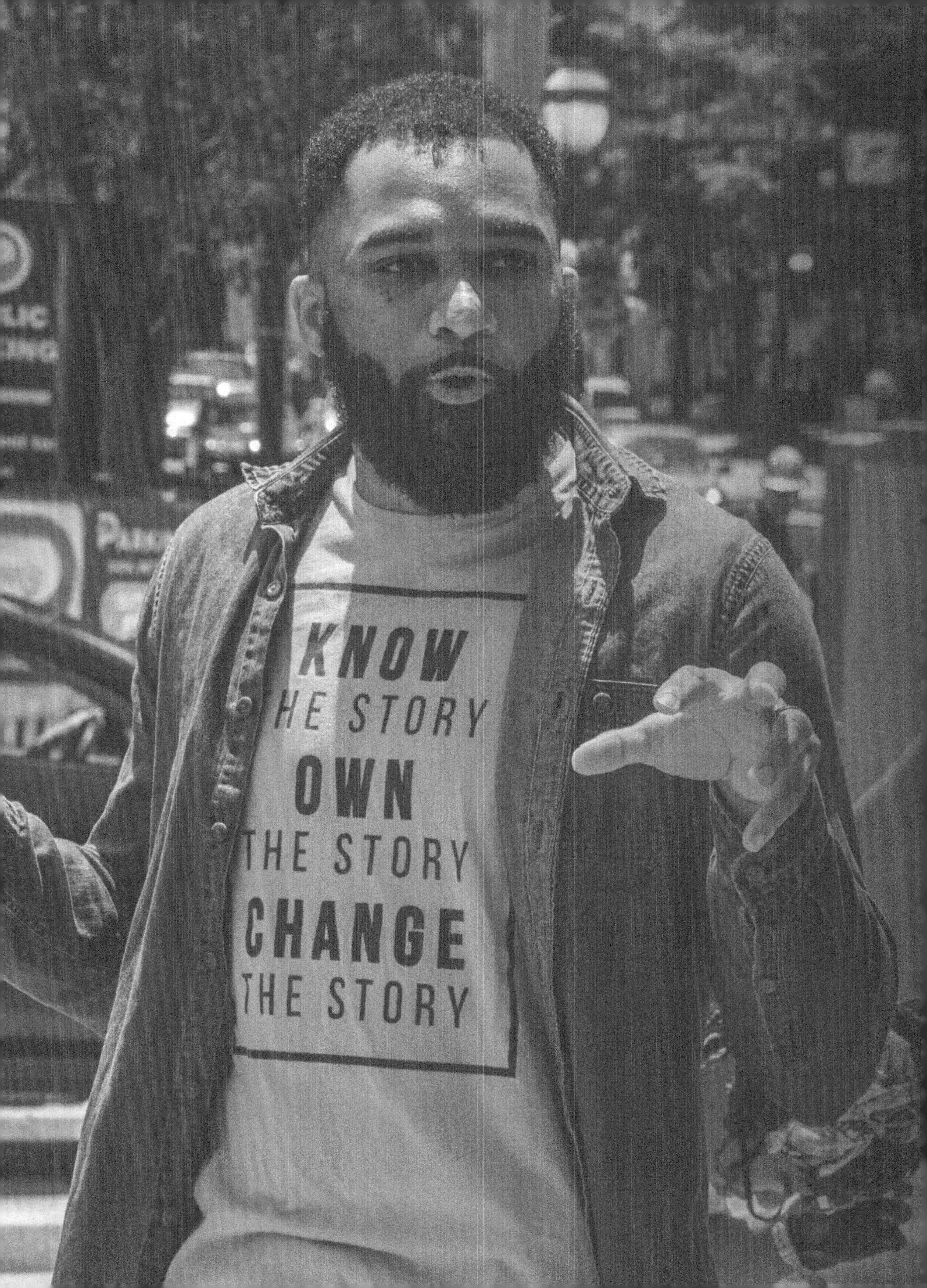
KNOW
THE STORY
OWN
THE STORY
CHANGE
THE STORY

Chapter 20
Ministering to the Hurting

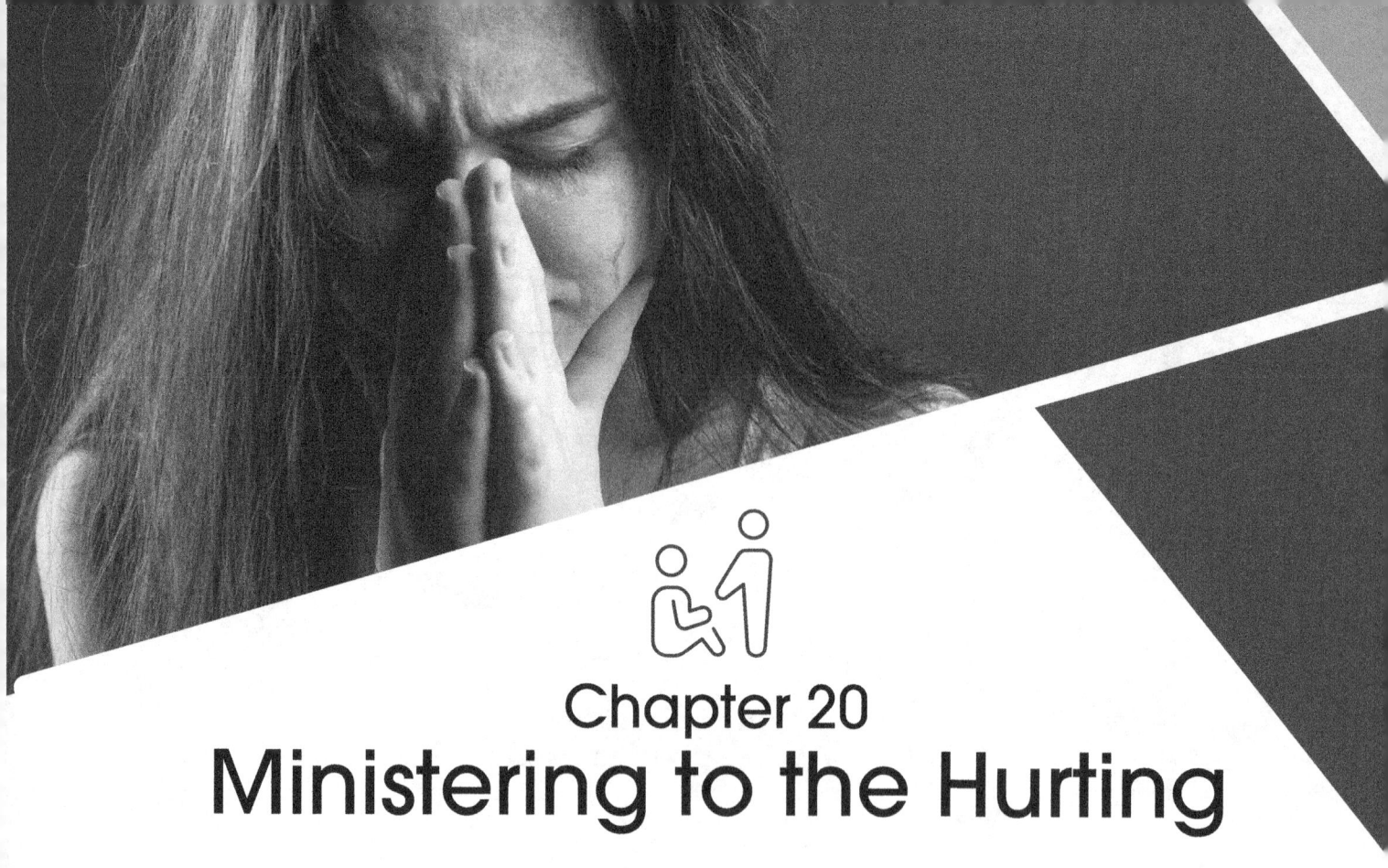

Occasionally, most people deal with some form of hurt in their lives. Unfortunately, many live a life where hurt and pain have totally overtaken them. It is seen in the way they live out their lives. Their actions will tell you how they are handling hurt and pain. Most times, their lifestyles scream, "I need help!"

Indicators That People Are Hurting

- Substance abuse
- Deep depression/suicidal thoughts
- Consistent emotional outbursts
- Repeated verbal attacks against others
- Abusive behavior or self-harm
- Victimized by abuse
- Disposition of anger
- Involvement in gangs
- Dressing to entice
- Promiscuity
- Anger at God
- Attitude of hopelessness

Challenges When Ministering to the Hurting

▶ Most people do not admit when they have a problem.

▶ They have listened to Satan for so long that they believe his lies ("But if our gospel be hid, it is hid to them that are lost: In whom the god of this world hath blinded the minds of them which believe not, lest the light of the glorious gospel of Christ, who is the image of God, should shine unto them" [2 Corinthians 4:3-4]).

▶ They have an "I've-tried-God-already" attitude.

▶ They do not see a way out.

▶ They're afraid to trust God.

▶ They have become addicted to their crutches in life.

▶ They blame everyone else for their issues.

▶ They do not believe that God loves them or cares for them.

▶ They are not ready to forgive others.

When evangelizing to this group of people, go to "the root" of the issue(s).

Read Mark 11:20-21 and take note of the tree being dried up from the roots. Every tree has roots and can survive and grow because of its roots. Do a quick study on the purpose of roots. Jot down what you find. Just like the roots provide life and sustainability for a tree, the core reason for a hurting person provides life and sustainability to their pain.

Read Proverbs 31:7. This Scripture will help you to understand why people turn to substance abuse. Consider the words *forget, poverty, remember,* and *misery* found in this verse.

Place a check beside each word in the category column that you believe most closely aligns with it.

	✔ MENTAL	✔ EMOTIONAL	✔ ENVIRONMENTAL
FORGET			
POVERTY			
REMEMBER			
MISERY			

Once you determine which category each word falls under, then you will have identified the reasons why hurting people turn to substance abuse and other things to find rest and peace for their souls.

Read Luke 4:18. You will clearly see that Jesus is able and willing to heal, deliver, and make people whole from hurts and pains. Use a good Bible concordance to define the words *brokenhearted* and *deliverance*.

Write down their meanings.

God has an answer for every challenge. Believers are to help the hurting see that Jesus is the only way out!

Armed with this information, explain how you will use it to help free people from Satan's grip on their lives and to cause them to receive healing from hurt and pain.

Note: It's imperative that you seek guidance from a trusted and experienced pastor or Christian counselor when helping others through mental, emotional, and environmental challenges. Ask leaders in your church for professional referrals. An excellent resource on this topic is *Hope for the Hurting* by Tony Evans (B&H Publishing Group, 2022).

Chapter 20
Ministering to the Hurting

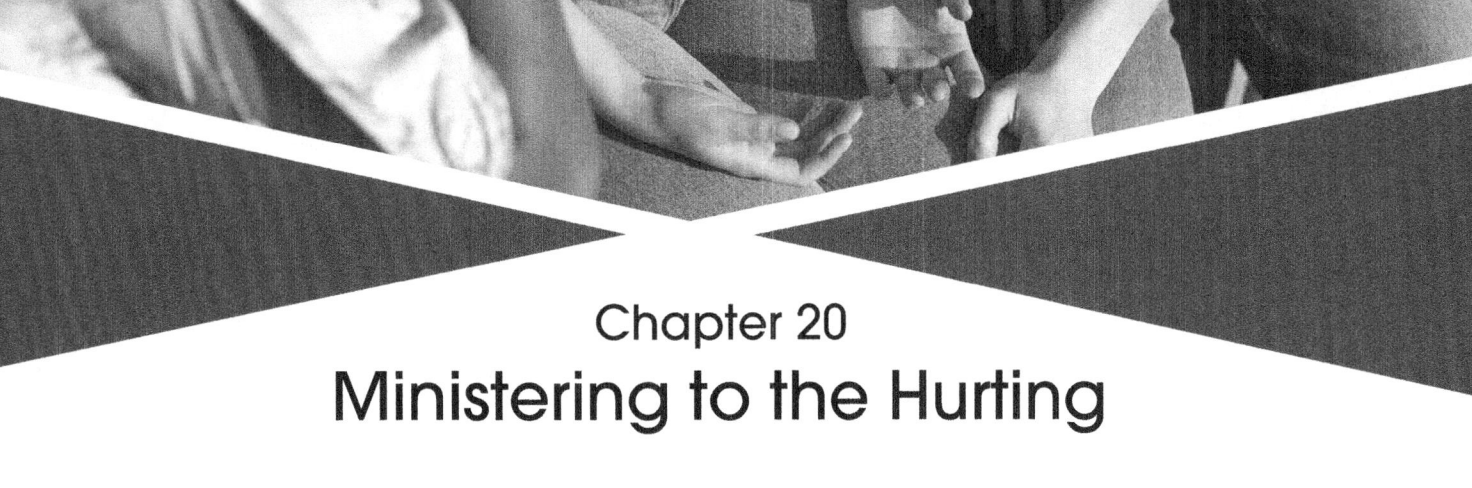

1. List six of the twelve indicators that people are hurting:

    a.

    b.

    c.

    d.

    e.

    f.

2. According to Proverbs 31:7, why do people turn to substance abuse for comfort?

3. When evangelizing hurt people, believers are to do what?

4. Believers are to help the hurting see that _____ is the only way out.

5. _____ of a person will tell you how they are handling hurt and pain.

Prayer, Healing, and Evangelism

In this Section:

▶ **The Power of Prayer and Evangelism**
When believers have a consistent prayer life, specifically praying in the Holy Spirit, evangelizing becomes easier.

▶ **The Link Between Healing and Evangelism**
Throughout Scripture, healing and the preaching of God's Word were constantly joined together.

▶ **Valuable Biblical Examples for Evangelizing**
The Bible has many valuable lessons that can be learned from others who have shared Christ with their generation.

▶ **Jesus: The Ultimate Example**
Scripture demonstrates Jesus' preaching and teaching the Gospel, as well as His healing people in the synagogues.

▶ **Evangelism Prayer for Believers**
A daily prayer over yourself to help you yield to "The Call" without intimidation!

Chapter 21
The Power of Prayer and Evangelism

Prayer and evangelism go hand-in-hand. When believers have a consistent prayer life, specifically praying in the Holy Spirit, evangelizing becomes easier.

Benefits of Daily Prayer

▶ Believers will become more sensitive to the voice of God.

▶ Believers will become more sensitive to the Holy Spirit's leading and guidance.

▶ Believers can easily follow the promptings and/or instructions of the Holy Spirit more often.

▶ Believers who follow the Holy Spirit while evangelizing will precisely meet the needs of the people to whom they are witnessing.

If you are not a person of prayer, write down how the benefits of prayer can help you in your personal life and with evangelizing.

If you are a person of prayer, write down how the benefits of prayer have helped you in your personal life.

Read the following Scriptures regarding prayer and determine what benefits are received from praying.

Romans 8:26-28
Likewise the Spirit also helpeth our infirmities: for we know not what we should pray for as we ought: but the Spirit itself maketh intercession for us with groanings which cannot be uttered. And he that searcheth the hearts knoweth what is the mind of the Spirit, because he maketh intercession for the saints according to the will of God. And we know that all things work together for good to them that love God, to them who are the called according to his purpose.

1 Peter 3:12
For the eyes of the Lord are over the righteous, and his ears are open unto their prayers: but the face of the Lord is against them that do evil.

Jude 20
But ye, beloved, building up yourselves on your most holy faith, praying in the Holy Ghost...

1 John 5:14-15
And this is the confidence that we have in him, that, if we ask any thing according to his will, he heareth us: And if we know that he hear us, whatsoever we ask, we know that we have the petitions that we desired of him.

Read the following Scriptures for the Holy Spirit's guidance and determine what benefits you receive from following the Holy Spirit.

Luke 12:12
For the Holy Ghost shall teach you in the same hour what ye ought to say.

John 16:13
Howbeit when he, the Spirit of truth, is come, he will guide you into all truth: for he shall not speak of himself; but whatsoever he shall hear, that shall he speak: and he will shew you things to come.

Acts 1:1-2
The former treatise have I made, O Theophilus, of all that Jesus began both to do and teach, Until the day in which he was taken up, after that he through the Holy Ghost had given commandments unto the apostles whom he had chosen...

Acts 8:29-30
Then the Spirit said unto Philip, Go near, and join thyself to this chariot. And Philip ran thither to him, and heard him read the prophet Esaias, and said, Understandest thou what thou readest?

Acts 16:6-7
Now when they had gone throughout Phrygia and the region of Galatia, and were forbidden of the Holy Ghost to preach the word in Asia, After they were come to Mysia, they assayed to go into Bithynia: but the Spirit suffered them not.

1 Peter 1:12
Unto whom it was revealed, that not unto themselves, but unto us they did minister the things, which are now reported unto you by them that have preached the gospel unto you with the Holy Ghost sent down from heaven; which things the angels desire to look into.

Read Jesus' prayer for believers to witness and write down your thoughts about the importance of you sharing Christ with others.

John 17:20-21
Neither pray I for these alone, but for them also which shall believe on me through their word; That they all may be one; as thou, Father, art in me, and I in thee, that they also may be one in us: that the world may believe that thou hast sent me.

Paul's Prayers for Effective Witnessing

Ephesians 6:18-20
Praying always with all prayer and supplication in the Spirit, and watching thereunto with all perseverance and supplication for all saints; And for me, that utterance may be given unto me, that I may open my mouth boldly, to make known the mystery of the gospel, For which I am an ambassador in bonds: that therein I may speak boldly, as I ought to speak.

2 Thessalonians 3:1-2
Finally, brethren, pray for us, that the word of the Lord may have free course, and be glorified, even as it is with you...

Paul's Prayer for an Opportunity to Witness

Colossians 4:3
Withal praying also for us, that God would open unto us a door of utterance, to speak the mystery of Christ, for which I am also in bonds...

Read the Scriptures of Jesus' example of prayer and evangelism and write down what happened in each portion of Scripture after Jesus spent time in prayer.

Matthew 14:22-23, 34-36
And straightway Jesus constrained his disciples to get into a ship, and to go before him unto the other side, while he sent the multitudes away. And when he had sent the multitudes away, he went up into a mountain apart to pray: and when the evening was come, he was there alone... And when they were gone over, they came into the land of Gennesaret. And when the men of that place had knowledge of him, they sent out into all that country round about, and brought unto him all that were diseased; And besought him that they might only touch the hem of his garment: and as many as touched were made perfectly whole.

Mark 1:35-42
And in the morning, rising up a great while before day, he went out, and departed into a solitary place, and there prayed. And Simon and they that were with him followed after him. And when they had found him, they said unto him, All men seek for thee. And he said unto them, Let us go into the next towns, that I may preach there also: for therefore came I forth. And he preached in their synagogues throughout all Galilee, and cast out devils. And there came a leper to him, beseeching him, and kneeling down to him, and saying unto him, If thou wilt, thou canst make me clean. And Jesus, moved with compassion, put forth his hand, and touched him, and saith unto him, I will; be thou clean. And as soon as he had spoken, immediately the leprosy departed from him, and he was cleansed.

Luke 6:12-13, 17-19
And it came to pass in those days, that he went out into a mountain to pray, and continued all night in prayer to God. And when it was day, he called unto him his disciples: and of them he chose twelve, whom also he named apostles; … And he came down with them, and stood in the plain, and the company of his disciples, and a great multitude of people out of all Judaea and Jerusalem, and from the sea coast of Tyre and Sidon, which came to hear him, and to be healed of their diseases; And they that were vexed with unclean spirits: and they were healed. And the whole multitude sought to touch him: for there went virtue out of him, and healed them all.

A Scripture That Can Be Used to Consistently Pray for the Lost

1 Timothy 2:1-4
I exhort therefore, that, first of all, supplications, prayers, intercessions, and giving of thanks, be made for all men; For kings, and for all that are in authority; that we may lead a quiet and peaceable life in all godliness and honesty. For this is good and acceptable in the sight of God our Saviour; Who will have all men to be saved, and to come unto the knowledge of the truth.

Scriptures That Can Be Used to Consistently Pray for Out-of-Fellowship and Backslidden Believers

Ephesians 1:16-19
Cease not to give thanks for you, making mention of you in my prayers; That the God of our Lord Jesus Christ, the Father of glory, may give unto you the spirit of wisdom and revelation in the knowledge of him: The eyes of your understanding being enlightened; that ye may know what is the hope of his calling, and what the riches of the glory of his inheritance in the saints, And what is the exceeding greatness of his power to us-ward who believe, according to the working of his mighty power...

Ephesians 6:18
Praying always with all prayer and supplication in the Spirit, and watching thereunto with all perseverance and supplication for all saints...

> *"The Holy Spirit knows exactly what to say to everyone to whom you will minister. Therefore, pray and receive His insight into people's lives."*
>
> —Evangelist Marie Diggs

Chapter 21
The Power of Prayer and Evangelism

1. What makes evangelizing easier?

2. What instructions does Jude 20 give to the believer?

3. Prayer and _____ go hand-in-hand.

4. What example did Jesus set for believers in Mark 1:35-42?

Chapter 22
The Link Between Healing and Evangelism

Healing and evangelism go hand-in-hand. Throughout Scripture, healing and the preaching of God's Word were constantly joined together.

During Jesus and His disciples' earthly ministry, they shared the love of God with many people and at times they also offered healing to those people. As a result, many were healed. Today, when evangelizing, it just makes sense to also lead people to God, the author of healing, sharing that Jesus was, and still is, the Healer! Indeed, God desires for all to be saved and for all to be healed! Furthermore, God expects us Christians to carry out the Great Commission seen in Mark 16:15-20, where Jesus commissions Christians to lay hands on the sick.

Read the Scriptures Linking Healing with Sharing the Word

Matthew 4:23
And Jesus went about all Galilee, teaching in their synagogues, and preaching the gospel of the kingdom, and healing all manner of sickness and all manner of disease among the people.

Here we see Jesus sharing the Word of God throughout all of Galilee, but I want you to note that His teaching and preaching were accompanied by healing. The Word comes to meet needs, and it is evident in this verse that people in His audience needed healing.

Matthew 15:21-28
Then Jesus went thence, and departed into the coasts of Tyre and Sidon. And, behold, a woman of Canaan came out of the same coasts, and cried unto him, saying, Have mercy on me, O Lord, thou son of David; my daughter is grievously vexed with a devil. But he answered her not a word. And his disciples came and besought him, saying, Send her away; for she crieth after us. But he answered and said, I am not sent but unto the lost sheep of the house of Israel. Then came she and worshipped him, saying, Lord, help me. But he answered and said, It is not meet to take the children's bread, and to cast it to dogs. And she said, Truth, Lord: yet the dogs eat of the crumbs which fall from their masters' table. Then Jesus answered and said unto her, O woman, great is thy faith: be it unto thee even as thou wilt. And her daughter was made whole from that very hour.

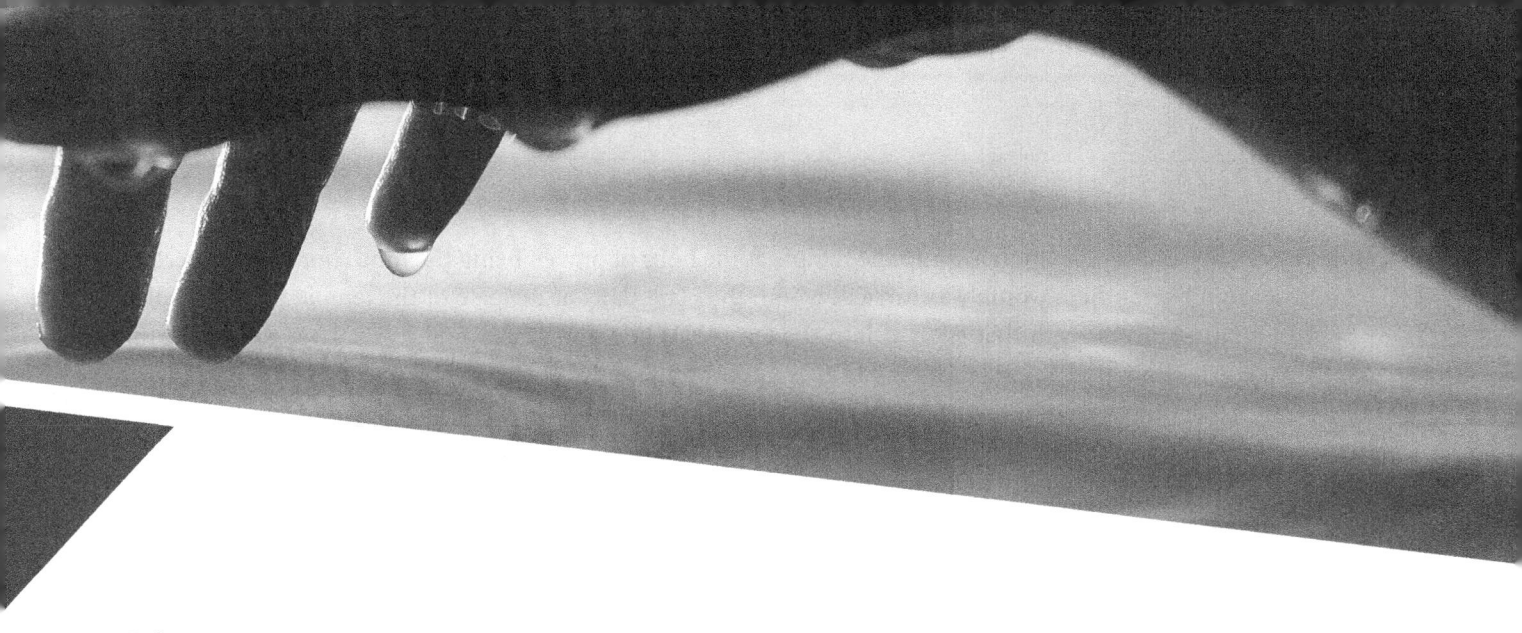

Luke 7:1-10

Now when he had ended all his sayings in the audience of the people, he entered into Capernaum. And a certain centurion's servant, who was dear unto him, was sick, and ready to die. And when he heard of Jesus, he sent unto him the elders of the Jews, beseeching him that he would come and heal his servant. And when they came to Jesus, they besought him instantly, saying, That he was worthy for whom he should do this: For he loveth our nation, and he hath built us a synagogue. Then Jesus went with them. And when he was now not far from the house, the centurion sent friends to him, saying unto him, Lord, trouble not thyself: for I am not worthy that thou shouldest enter under my roof: Wherefore neither thought I myself worthy to come unto thee: but say in a word, and my servant shall be healed. For I also am a man set under authority, having under me soldiers, and I say unto one, Go, and he goeth; and to another, Come, and he cometh; and to my servant, Do this, and he doeth it. When Jesus heard these things, he marvelled at him, and turned him about, and said unto the people that followed him, I say unto you, I have not found so great faith, no, not in Israel. And they that were sent, returning to the house, found the servant whole that had been sick.

Luke 9:11

And the people, when they knew it, followed him: and he received them, and spake unto them of the kingdom of God, and healed them that had need of healing.

> *Once again, we see Jesus ministering the Word of God and ministering healing to those in need of healing.*

Acts 2:36-38, 40-43, 47

Therefore let all the house of Israel know assuredly, that God hath made that same Jesus, whom ye have crucified, both Lord and Christ. Now when they heard this, they were pricked in their heart, and said unto Peter and to the rest of the apostles, Men and brethren, what shall we do? Then Peter said unto them, Repent, and be baptized every one of you in the name of Jesus Christ for the remission of sins, and ye shall receive the gift of the Holy Ghost. …And with many other words did he testify and exhort, saying, Save yourselves from this untoward generation. Then they that gladly received his word were baptized: and the same day there were added unto them about three thousand souls. And they continued stedfastly in the apostles' doctrine and fellowship, and in breaking of bread, and in prayers. And fear came upon every soul: and many wonders and signs were done by the apostles. Praising God, and having favour with all the people. And the Lord added to the church daily such as should be saved.

> *Not only did healing accompany Jesus' preaching of the Gospel, but it also accompanied the apostles' preaching of the Gospel. The Bible says, "many wonders and signs were done by the apostles." Undoubtedly, some of these wonders and signs were the healing of the sick, as you will read in the following Scriptural references.*

Acts 3:1-10

Now Peter and John went up together into the temple at the hour of prayer, being the ninth hour. And a certain man lame from his mother's womb was carried, whom they laid daily at the gate of the temple which is called Beautiful, to ask alms of them that entered into the temple; Who seeing Peter and John about to go into the temple asked an alms. And Peter, fastening his eyes upon him with John, said, Look on us. And he gave heed unto them, expecting to receive something of them. Then Peter said, Silver and gold have I none; but such as I have give I thee: In the name of Jesus Christ of Nazareth rise up and walk. And he took him by the right hand, and lifted him up: and immediately his feet and ankle bones received strength. And he leaping up stood, and walked, and entered with them into the temple, walking, and leaping, and praising God. And all the people saw him walking and praising God: And they knew that it was he which sat for alms at the Beautiful gate of the temple: and they were filled with wonder and amazement at that which had happened unto him.

Acts 5:12-15

And by the hands of the apostles were many signs and wonders wrought among the people; (and they were all with one accord in Solomon's porch. And of the rest durst no man join himself to them: but the people magnified them. And believers were the more added to the Lord, multitudes both of men and women.) Insomuch that they brought forth the sick into the streets, and laid them on beds and couches, that at the least the shadow of Peter passing by might overshadow some of them.

Acts 8:5-8

Then Philip went down to the city of Samaria, and preached Christ unto them. And the people with one accord gave heed unto those things which Philip spake, hearing and seeing the miracles which he did. For unclean spirits, crying with loud voice, came out of many that were possessed with them: and many taken with palsies, and that were lame, were healed. And there was great joy in that city.

> *Here we have Philip, the Evangelist, preaching the Gospel of Christ to a city of Gentiles. Accompanying his preaching were miracles, and amongst the miracles noted was the healing of those with paralysis. Hopefully, by now, you see that God does not just want to heal man's sinned-filled soul, but every part of him – spirit, soul, and body. And that is why there is a link between sharing the Word and healing.*

Acts 10:38

How God anointed Jesus of Nazareth with the Holy Ghost and with power: who went about doing good, and healing all that were oppressed of the devil; for God was with him.

> *This verse tells us that Jesus was anointed with the Holy Ghost and with power, and He used this power to heal the sick. Accordingly, you and I have been anointed by the Holy Ghost and with power (Acts 1:8), and we have been commissioned to do the works of Christ (John 14:12). Therefore, every believer sharing the Gospel should expect to be used by God to minister healing to the sick.*

Acts 28:8

And it came to pass, that the father of Publius lay sick of a fever and of a bloody flux: to whom Paul entered in, and prayed, and laid his hands on him, and healed him.

> *Just as Paul laid hands on Publius' father in faith, and he received his healing, we must have the same boldness and faith to do the same when we see people afflicted in their bodies with sickness and disease.*

Healing: A Provision God Made for Humankind

Healing is the calling card for the lost. Some people call it the "dinner bell for the lost." When a non-believer hears and receives that Jesus is willing to heal them, most often they take what is being offered.

Even throughout the Gospels, Jesus and His disciples ministered healing to many people. None of them, however, were saved, because Jesus had not yet given His life as a sacrifice on the cross of Calvary to pay for humankind's sin, nor for the provision of healing.

Additionally, in Jesus' earthly ministry, God had anointed Him with the Holy Ghost and with power and had instructed Him to heal all that were oppressed by the Devil according to Acts 10:38. Initially Jesus was sent to the Jewish people, and healing was "the children's bread"; however, there were instances where God allowed non-Jewish people to receive healing as seen with the Syrophoenician Woman's daughter in Matthew 15:21-28 and the Samaritan leper seen in Luke 17:11-16. Also, later in the Scripture, God revealed to the disciples that His plan was to extend the Gospel to all people. Healing is a part of the Gospel of salvation.

Lastly, Hebrews 13:8 tells us that Jesus Christ is the same yesterday, and today, and forever! Thus, in the same way, Jesus' healing provision is available for anyone today who would receive it.

When Can a Person Be Healed by Jesus?

- ▶ Before a person is saved
- ▶ At the time a person gets saved
- ▶ After a person is saved

Healing Is Included in Salvation

Read Romans 10:8-10, 13 and you will find the blueprint for how to get saved. Now write down the steps shared for a person to receive the gift of salvation as seen in Romans 10:8-10, 13.

Note: From my studies I have found that the word *saved* in the Greek language in the above portion of Scripture means to preserve, rescue, save, and heal. Thus, healing is clearly a part of the salvation package.

When Jesus died, His suffering and death paid for more than our sins. According to Isaiah 53:4, He carried man's sickness and pain, and in verse 5, He was tormented for man's rebellion or transgression and crushed for man's offense or iniquities.

In Galatians 3:13-14, He became a curse to redeem humankind from the curse of the law which includes sin, sickness, and disease, lack and poverty, and spiritual death. Lastly, according to 1 Peter 2:24, He has borne our sins (the curse) in His own body on the cross so that we would have the opportunity to partake of every blessing received through Jesus Christ.

Now write down the steps shared for a person to receive the gift of salvation as seen in Romans 10:8-10, 13.

Read the Scriptures below regarding healing, and meditate on how good God is to offer healing as a gift to everyone (saved and unsaved).

Genesis 20:17
So Abraham prayed unto God: and God healed Abimelech, and his wife, and his maidservants; and they bare children.

> *Here we see God's provision of healing long before Jesus died to give everyone the opportunity to partake of healing.*

Psalm 103:1-4
Bless the LORD, O my soul: and all that is within me, bless his holy name. Bless the LORD, O my soul, and forget not all his benefits: Who forgiveth all thine iniquities; who healeth all thy diseases; Who redeemeth thy life from destruction; who crowneth thee with lovingkindness and tender mercies...

> *This verse tells us that it is a characteristic of God to pardon sin and to heal.*

Isaiah 53:4-5

Surely he hath borne our griefs, and carried our sorrows: yet we did esteem him stricken, smitten of God, and afflicted. But he was wounded for our transgressions, he was bruised for our iniquities: the chastisement of our peace was upon him; and with his stripes we are healed.

Isaiah 53:10

Yet it pleased the LORD to bruise him; he hath put him to grief: when thou shalt make his soul an offering for sin, he shall see his seed, he shall prolong his days, and the pleasure of the LORD shall prosper in his hand.

> *Once again, we see in Scripture that God desires for people to receive healing. He took delight and great pleasure in putting Jesus to grief, meaning making Him sick and weak so that humankind would have the opportunity to be made whole.*

Galatians 3:13-14

Christ hath redeemed us from the curse of the law, being made a curse for us: for it is written, Cursed is every one that hangeth on a tree: That the blessing of Abraham might come on the Gentiles through Jesus Christ; that we might receive the promise of the Spirit through faith.

1 Peter 2:24

Who his own self bare our sins in his own body on the tree, that we, being dead to sins, should live unto righteousness: by whose stripes ye were healed.

> *"Healing is God's will. It is an act of His volition and His great love for humankind. Ask yourself this question, 'Since God provided the good gift of healing for all humankind, what other good things would man receive if they partake of the gift of salvation extended to them by God?'"*
>
> —Evangelist Marie Diggs

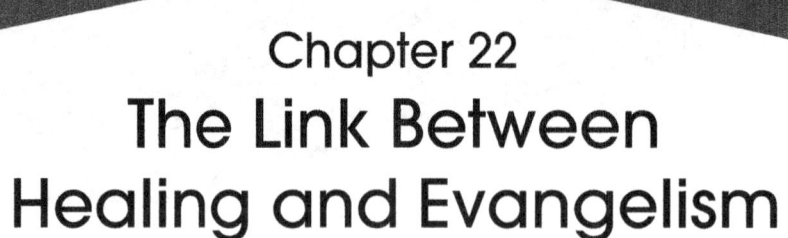

Chapter 22
The Link Between Healing and Evangelism

1. What can be used as a gateway to witness the Gospel?

2. Healing and _____ go hand-in-hand.

3. God made healing a provision for whom?

4. Does a person have to be saved before they can be healed?

5. When can a person be healed by Jesus?

   a.

   b.

   c.

6. In Romans 10:8-10, 13 what does the word *saved* mean in this portion of the Scripture?

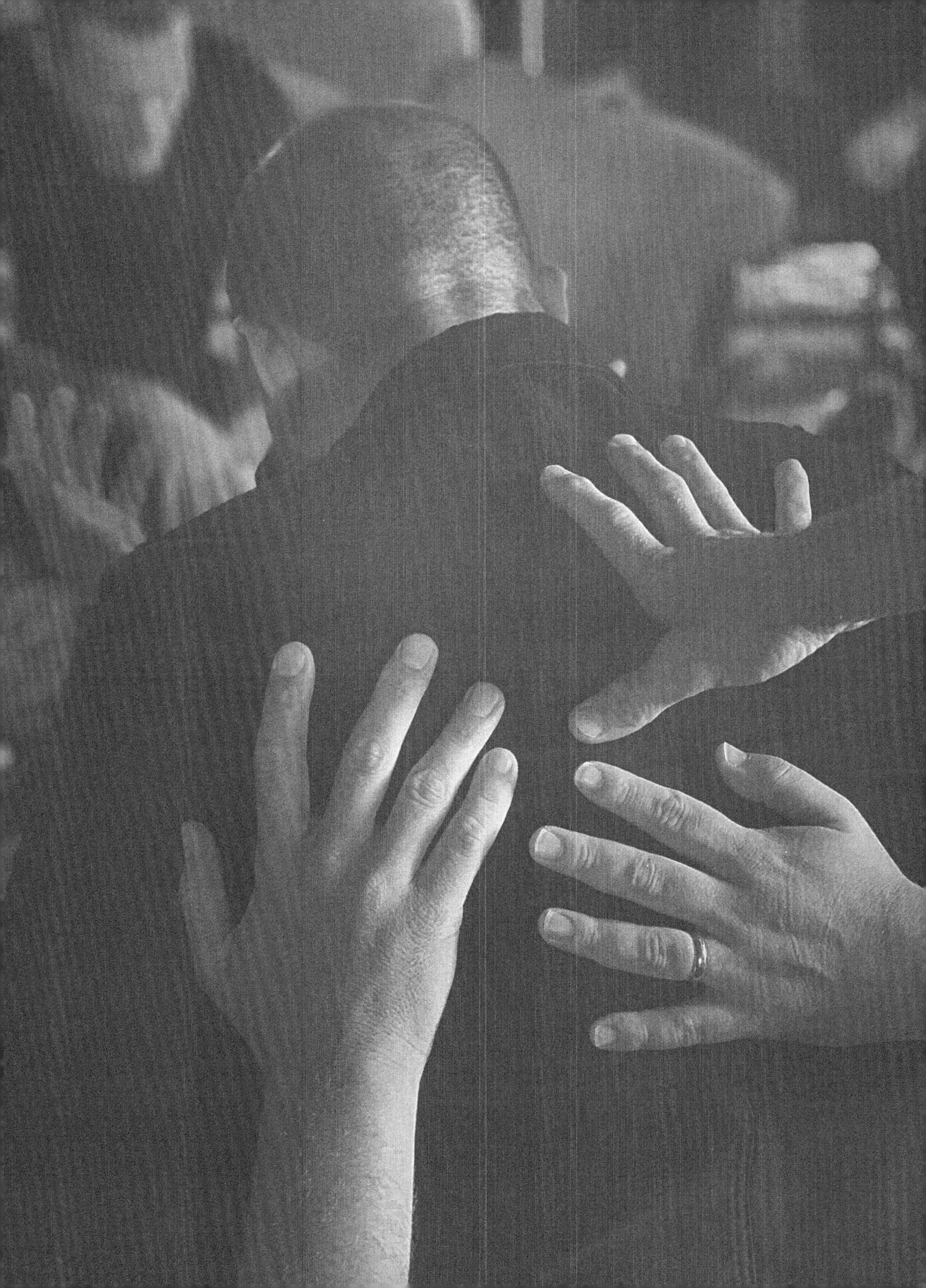

Chapter 23
Valuable Biblical Examples for Evangelizing

The Bible has many valuable lessons that can be learned from others who have shared Christ with their generation. Take the time to read each scriptural reference given in this chapter and jot down the lesson learned from each account. I encourage you to use a Bible concordance to define some of the words with the Scriptures listed in this section as it will only enhance your time of study.

2 Corinthians 5:17-20
God identifies what believers should share when witnessing.

John 3:1-21
Jesus' witness to Nicodemus

John 4:4-28, 39
Jesus' witness to the woman at the well

John 4:39, 42
The woman at the well's witness of Jesus

John 4:40-41
Jesus' witness to the men of Samaria

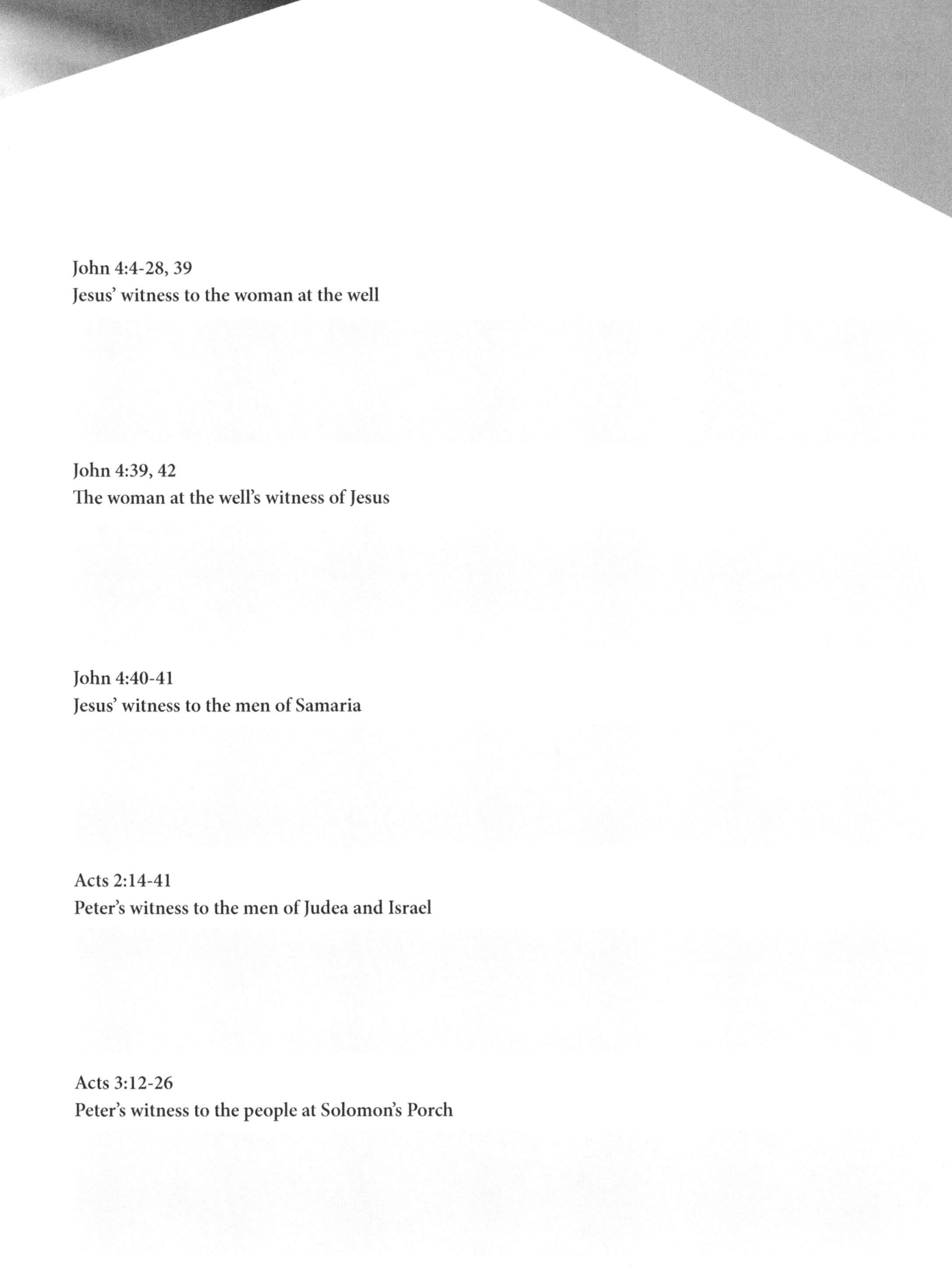

Acts 2:14-41
Peter's witness to the men of Judea and Israel

Acts 3:12-26
Peter's witness to the people at Solomon's Porch

Acts 4:5-14
Peter's bold witness

Acts 5:27-32
Peter and the other apostles' witness of Jesus

Acts 8:5-7
Phillip's witness to the Samaritans

Acts 8:26-37
Phillip's witness to an Ethiopian man

Acts 10:28-47
Peter's witness to Cornelius, to his family, and to his close friends

Acts 13:44-49
Paul's witness to almost a whole city

Acts 14:6-10
Paul's witness to a lame man

Acts 17:1-3, 6
Paul's witness in Thessalonica

Acts 17:16-34
Paul's witness in Athens

Acts 22:3-23
Paul's witness before a huge crowd of people in Jerusalem

Acts 26:4-28
Paul's witness before King Agrippa

Acts 28:20-31
Paul's witness in prison

Chapter 24
Jesus: The Ultimate Example

Every believer should strive to be like Jesus! Many Scriptures demonstrate Jesus' preaching and teaching the Gospel, as well as His healing people in the synagogues. However, Jesus preached, taught, and healed them in other places as well:

- ▶ In His own house
- ▶ In other people's houses
- ▶ On the streets and in communities
- ▶ On mountainsides
- ▶ By the seaside
- ▶ By the highway
- ▶ In the marketplace
- ▶ In various open areas

Therefore, in like manner, believers are to follow Jesus' example by preaching and teaching the Gospel, and by allowing God to heal people through them in the various places that they go throughout their day.

- At the beauty salon or the barber shop
- While waiting for a scheduled appointment at a doctor's office or at school
- While shopping at a mall or while shopping for groceries
- At a place of entertainment like the movies, a park, or a ball game, etc.
- At a restaurant
- While using public transportation
- At the gym or at an exercise class
- At school before or after class
- At family gatherings
- Before or after work and during lunch breaks

The Bible tells us that when a person professes that they abide in Jesus (meaning that they are born again and living in fellowship with Him), they should conduct their lives and behaviors in the same manner as He did. Scripture is clear that Jesus received His "way of life" from His Father and that He only did what His Father told or showed Him to do (see John 8:28-29, 1 John 2:6).

Therefore, a believer's way of life should mimic Jesus' life of ministry. Jesus' life clearly demonstrated that *evangelizing is best done through conversational and relational means.*

Jesus' Preaching and Healing in the Streets

Matthew Chapter 5 through Chapter 7
The Sermon on the Mount

Mark 4:1-2
And he began again to teach by the sea side: and there was gathered unto him a great multitude, so that he entered into a ship, and sat in the sea; and the whole multitude was by the sea on the land. And he taught them many things by parables, and said unto them in his doctrine...

Mark 7:31-35
And again, departing from the coasts of Tyre and Sidon, he came unto the sea of Galilee, through the midst of the coasts of Decapolis. And they bring unto him one that was deaf, and had an impediment in his speech; and they beseech him to put his hand upon him. And he took him aside from the multitude, and put his fingers into his ears, and he spit, and touched his tongue; And looking up to heaven, he sighed, and saith unto him, Ephphatha, that is, Be opened. And straightway his ears were opened, and the string of his tongue was loosed, and he spake plain.

Luke 6:17-19
And he came down with them, and stood in the plain, and the company of his disciples, and a great multitude of people out of all Judaea and Jerusalem, and from the sea coast of Tyre and Sidon, which came to hear him, and to be healed of their diseases; And they that were vexed with unclean spirits: and they were healed. And the whole multitude sought to touch him: for there went virtue out of him, and healed them all.

John 4:6-7, 13-14, 29
Now Jacob's well was there. Jesus therefore, being wearied with his journey, sat thus on the well: and it was about the sixth hour. There cometh a woman of Samaria to draw water: Jesus saith unto her, Give me to drink. ... Jesus answered and said unto her, Whosoever drinketh of this water shall thirst again: But whosoever drinketh of the water that I shall give him shall never thirst; but the water that I shall give him shall be in him a well of water springing up into everlasting life. ... Come, see a man, which told me all things that ever I did: is not this the Christ?

Jesus' Preaching in the Community

Mark 1:37-38
And when they had found him, they said unto him, All men seek for thee. And he said unto them, Let us go into the next towns, that I may preach there also: for therefore came I forth.

Jesus' Preaching and Healing in His House

Mark 2:1-4
And again he entered into Capernaum after some days; and it was noised that he was in the house. And straightway many were gathered together, insomuch that there was no room to receive them, no, not so much as about the door: and he preached the word unto them. And they come unto him, bringing one sick of the palsy, which was borne of four. And when they could not come nigh unto him for the press, they uncovered the roof where he was: and when they had broken it up, they let down the bed wherein the sick of the palsy lay.

Jesus' Healing in the Community

Matthew 8:16
When the even was come, they brought unto him many that were possessed with devils: and he cast out the spirits with his word, and healed all that were sick...

Luke 4:40
Now when the sun was setting, all they that had any sick with divers diseases brought them unto him; and he laid his hands on every one of them, and healed them.

John 5:2-3, 5-6, 8-9
Now there is at Jerusalem by the sheep market a pool, which is called in the Hebrew tongue Bethesda, having five porches. In these lay a great multitude of impotent folk, of blind, halt, withered, waiting for the moving of the water. ... And a certain man was there, which had an infirmity thirty and eight years. When Jesus saw him lie, and knew that he had been now a long time in that case, he saith unto him, Wilt thou be made whole? ... Jesus saith unto him, Rise, take up thy bed, and walk. And immediately the man was made whole, and took up his bed, and walked: and on the same day was the sabbath.

Jesus' Healing in Houses

Matthew 9:23-25
And when Jesus came into the ruler's house, and saw the minstrels and the people making a noise, He said unto them, Give place: for the maid is not dead, but sleepeth. And they laughed him to scorn. But when the people were put forth, he went in, and took her by the hand, and the maid arose.

Matthew 9:27-30
And when Jesus departed thence, two blind men followed him, crying, and saying, Thou Son of David, have mercy on us. And when he was come into the house, the blind men came to him: and Jesus saith unto them, Believe ye that I am able to do this? They said unto him, Yea, Lord. Then touched he their eyes, saying, According to your faith be it unto you. And their eyes were opened; and Jesus straitly charged them, saying, See that no man know it.

Luke 4:38-39
And he arose out of the synagogue, and entered into Simon's house. And Simon's wife's mother was taken with a great fever; and they besought him for her. And he stood over her, and rebuked the fever; and it left her: and immediately she arose and ministered unto them.

Luke 14:1-4
And it came to pass, as he went into the house of one of the chief Pharisees to eat bread on the sabbath day, that they watched him. And, behold, there was a certain man before him which had the dropsy. And Jesus answering spake unto the lawyers and Pharisees, saying, Is it lawful to heal on the sabbath day? And they held their peace. And he took him, and healed him, and let him go....

Jesus' Healing in the Streets

Matthew 8:1-3

When he was come down from the mountain, great multitudes followed him. And, behold, there came a leper and worshipped him, saying, Lord, if thou wilt, thou canst make me clean. And Jesus put forth his hand, and touched him, saying, I will; be thou clean. And immediately his leprosy was cleansed.

Matthew 8:28, 32

And when he was come to the other side into the country of the Gergesenes, there met him two possessed with devils, coming out of the tombs, exceeding fierce, so that no man might pass by that way.… And he said unto them, Go. And when they were come out, they went into the herd of swine: and, behold, the whole herd of swine ran violently down a steep place into the sea, and perished in the waters.

Matthew 9:20, 22

And, behold, a woman, which was diseased with an issue of blood twelve years, came behind him, and touched the hem of his garment. … But Jesus turned him about, and when he saw her, he said, Daughter, be of good comfort; thy faith hath made thee whole. And the woman was made whole from that hour.

Mark 8:22-25

And he cometh to Bethsaida; and they bring a blind man unto him, and besought him to touch him. And he took the blind man by the hand, and led him out of the town; and when he had spit on his eyes, and put his hands upon him, he asked him if he saw ought. And he looked up, and said, I see men as trees, walking. After that he put his hands again upon his eyes, and made him look up: and he was restored, and saw every man clearly.

Mark 10:46-47, 51-52

And they came to Jericho: and as he went out of Jericho with his disciples and a great number of people, blind Bartimaeus, the son of Timaeus, sat by the highway side begging. And when he heard that it was Jesus of Nazareth, he began to cry out, and say, Jesus, thou Son of David, have mercy on me. … And Jesus answered and said unto him, What wilt thou that I should do unto thee? The blind man said unto him, Lord, that I might receive my sight. And Jesus said unto him, Go thy way; thy faith hath made thee whole. And immediately he received his sight, and followed Jesus in the way.

Luke 9:37-39, 42

And it came to pass, that on the next day, when they were come down from the hill, much people met him. And, behold, a man of the company cried out, saying, Master, I beseech thee, look upon my son: for he is mine only child. And, lo, a spirit taketh him, and he suddenly crieth out; and it teareth him that he foameth again, and bruising him hardly departeth from him. … And as he was yet a coming, the devil threw him down, and tare him. And Jesus rebuked the unclean spirit, and healed the child, and delivered him again to his father.

Luke 17:11-14

And it came to pass, as he went to Jerusalem, that he passed through the midst of Samaria and Galilee. And as he entered into a certain village, there met him ten men that were lepers, which stood afar off: And they lifted up their voices, and said, Jesus, Master, have mercy on us. And when he saw them, he said unto them, Go shew yourselves unto the priests. And it came to pass, that, as they went, they were cleansed.

Luke 22:50-51

And one of them smote the servant of the high priest, and cut off his right ear. And Jesus answered and said, Suffer ye thus far. And he touched his ear, and healed him.

John 8:59—9:1, 6-7

Then took they up stones to cast at him: but Jesus hid himself, and went out of the temple, going through the midst of them, and so passed by. And as Jesus passed by, he saw a man which was blind from his birth. … When he had thus spoken, he spat on the ground, and made clay of the spittle, and he anointed the eyes of the blind man with the clay, And said unto him, Go, wash in the pool of Siloam, (which is by interpretation, Sent.) He went his way therefore, and washed, and came seeing.

Make a list of the places where you will begin to witness to others. Also, write down how witnessing in these areas will impact those who may be able to hear you witnessing to others.

"A Christian's life should mimic Jesus' life. Thus, we should exist to please the Father and to share Christ with the world."

—Evangelist Marie Diggs

Chapter 24
Jesus: The Ultimate Example

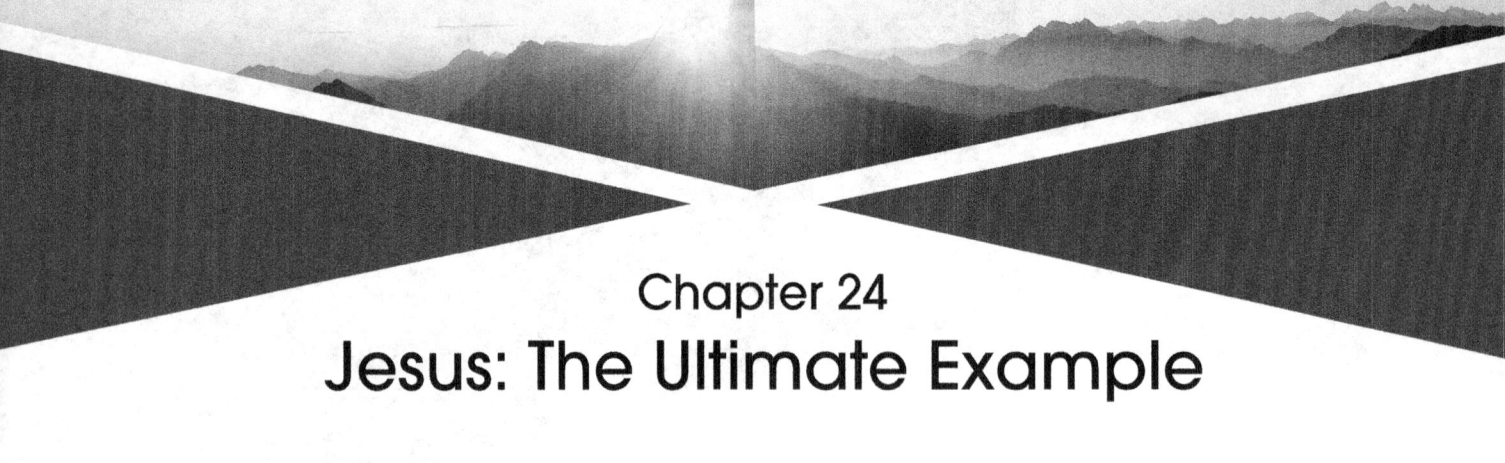

1. How are believers to follow Jesus' example?

2. If believers are to be like Jesus and follow His example, where should they be preaching, teaching, and healing?

3. Every believer should strive to be like whom?

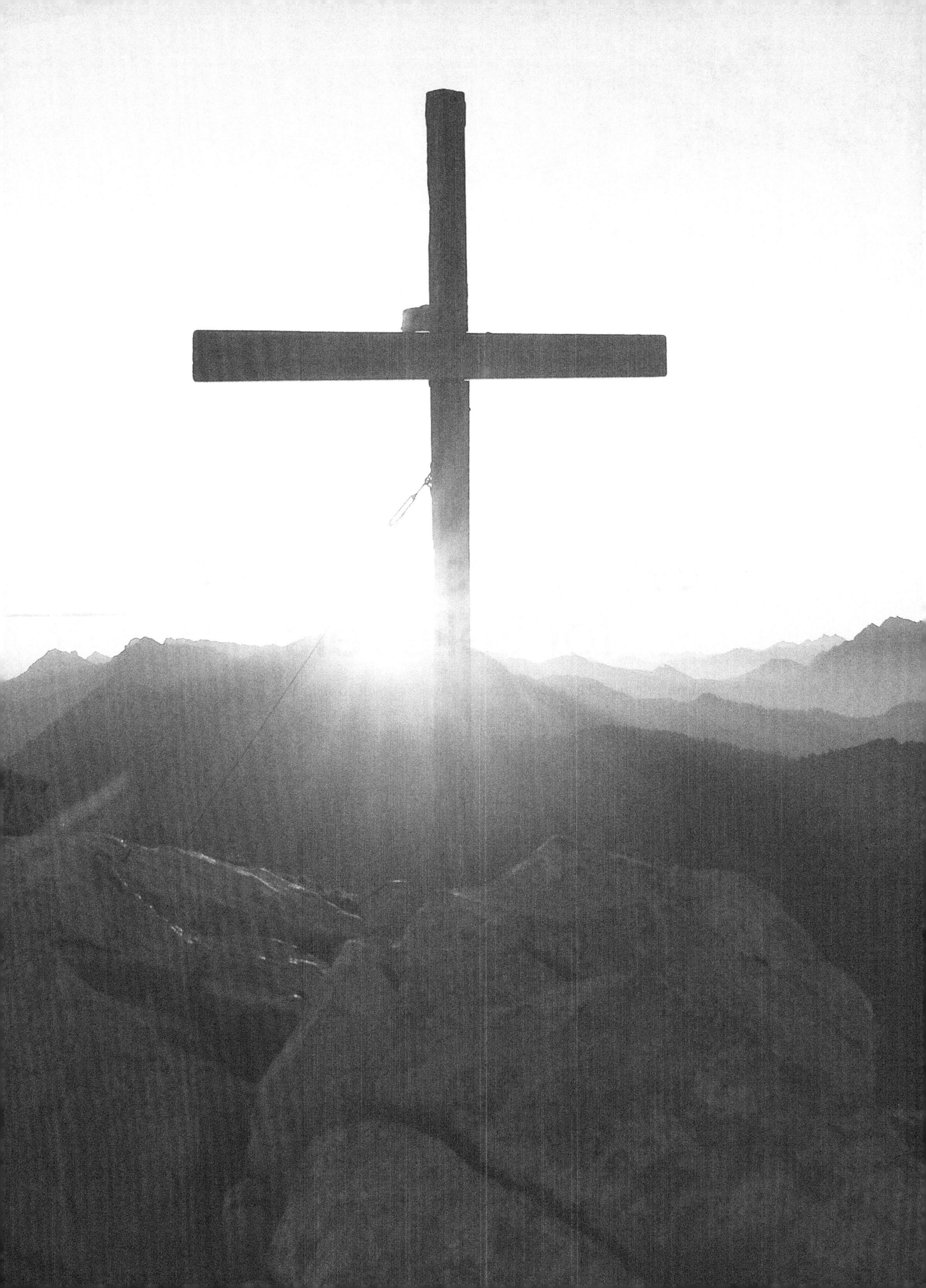

Chapter 25
Evangelism Prayer for Believers

Below is an evangelism prayer. Daily pray this prayer over yourself to help you to yield to The Call without intimidation!

Dear Father,

In Jesus' Name, I choose to take my rightful place in the body of Christ as an ambassador for Christ! I purpose within my heart to increase your family by sharing God's good news about Jesus with people everywhere I go.

I recognize I am never alone when I preach the Gospel. Therefore, I am in expectation of the Holy Spirit's guidance and Jesus' confirming the word that I boldly speak in His authority.

I fully expect people to be saved, brought back into right fellowship with God, and to be healed of sickness and disease. I anticipate signs and miracles to follow me as a believer and for people to be totally freed from Satan's bondage.

"For I am not ashamed of the gospel of Christ: for it is the power of God unto salvation to every one that believeth; to the Jew first, and also to the Greek" (Romans 1:16).

In His name, I pray, Amen.

Chapter 25
Evangelism Prayer for Believers

1. Are you ever alone when you share the Gospel of Jesus Christ?

2. When believers share the Gospel of Jesus Christ, who guides them and who confirms the word of truth that they speak?

3. Who is with you as you share the Gospel of Jesus Christ our Lord and Savior?

Benefits of Evangelism

In this Section:

▶ **Scriptures to Build Bold Faith**
You will find a list of Scriptures to help you to become a bold witness for Christ.

▶ **The Joys & Promises of Evangelizing**
God has promises waiting for the believer who will boldly and unashamedly step up and share Christ with the lost.

Chapter 26
Scriptures to Build Bold Faith

In this chapter, you will find a list of Scriptures that, when read aloud and meditated upon, will help you to become a bold witness for Christ. Read these Scriptures aloud and meditate on them one by one until a boldness to be a daily witness of Christ rises within your heart and soul!

Proverbs 28:1
The wicked flee when no man pursueth: but the righteous are bold as a lion.

John 7:26
But, lo, he speaketh boldly, and they say nothing unto him. Do the rulers know indeed that this is the very Christ?

Acts 4:13
Now when they saw the boldness of Peter and John, and perceived that they were unlearned and ignorant men, they marvelled; and they took knowledge of them, that they had been with Jesus.

Acts 4:29
And now, Lord, behold their threatenings: and grant unto thy servants, that with all boldness they may speak thy word...

Acts 4:31
And when they had prayed, the place was shaken where they were assembled together; and they were all filled with the Holy Ghost, and they spake the word of God with boldness.

Acts 9:27
But Barnabas took him, and brought him to the apostles, and declared unto them how he had seen the Lord in the way, and that he had spoken to him, and how he had preached boldly at Damascus in the name of Jesus.

Acts 9:29
And he spake boldly in the name of the Lord Jesus, and disputed against the Grecians: but they went about to slay him.

Acts 13:46
Then Paul and Barnabas waxed bold, and said, It was necessary that the word of God should first have been spoken to you: but seeing ye put it from you, and judge yourselves unworthy of everlasting life, lo, we turn to the Gentiles.

Acts 14:3
Long time therefore abode they speaking boldly in the Lord, which gave testimony unto the word of his grace, and granted signs and wonders to be done by their hands.

Acts 18:26
And he began to speak boldly in the synagogue: whom when Aquila and Priscilla had heard, they took him unto them, and expounded unto him the way of God more perfectly.

Acts 19:8
And he went into the synagogue, and spake boldly for the space of three months, disputing and persuading the things concerning the kingdom of God.

Ephesians 6:19
And for me, that utterance may be given unto me, that I may open my mouth boldly, to make known the mystery of the gospel...

Ephesians 6:20
For which I am an ambassador in bonds: that therein I may speak boldly, as I ought to speak.

Philippians 1:14
And many of the brethren in the Lord, waxing confident by my bonds, are much more bold to speak the word without fear.

I Thessalonians 2:2
But even after that we had suffered before, and were shamefully entreated, as ye know, at Philippi, we were bold in our God to speak unto you the gospel of God with much contention.

1 Peter 3:15
But sanctify the Lord God in your hearts: and be ready always to give an answer to every man that asketh you a reason of the hope that is in you with meekness and fear...

Jude 23
And others save with fear, pulling them out of the fire; hating even the garment spotted by the flesh.

Chapter 26
Scriptures to Build Bold Faith

1. The righteous (believers, children of God) are as bold as

2. Write out the Scriptures below, memorize them, and speak them over yourself daily.

    a. Ephesians 6:19

    b. Proverbs 28:1

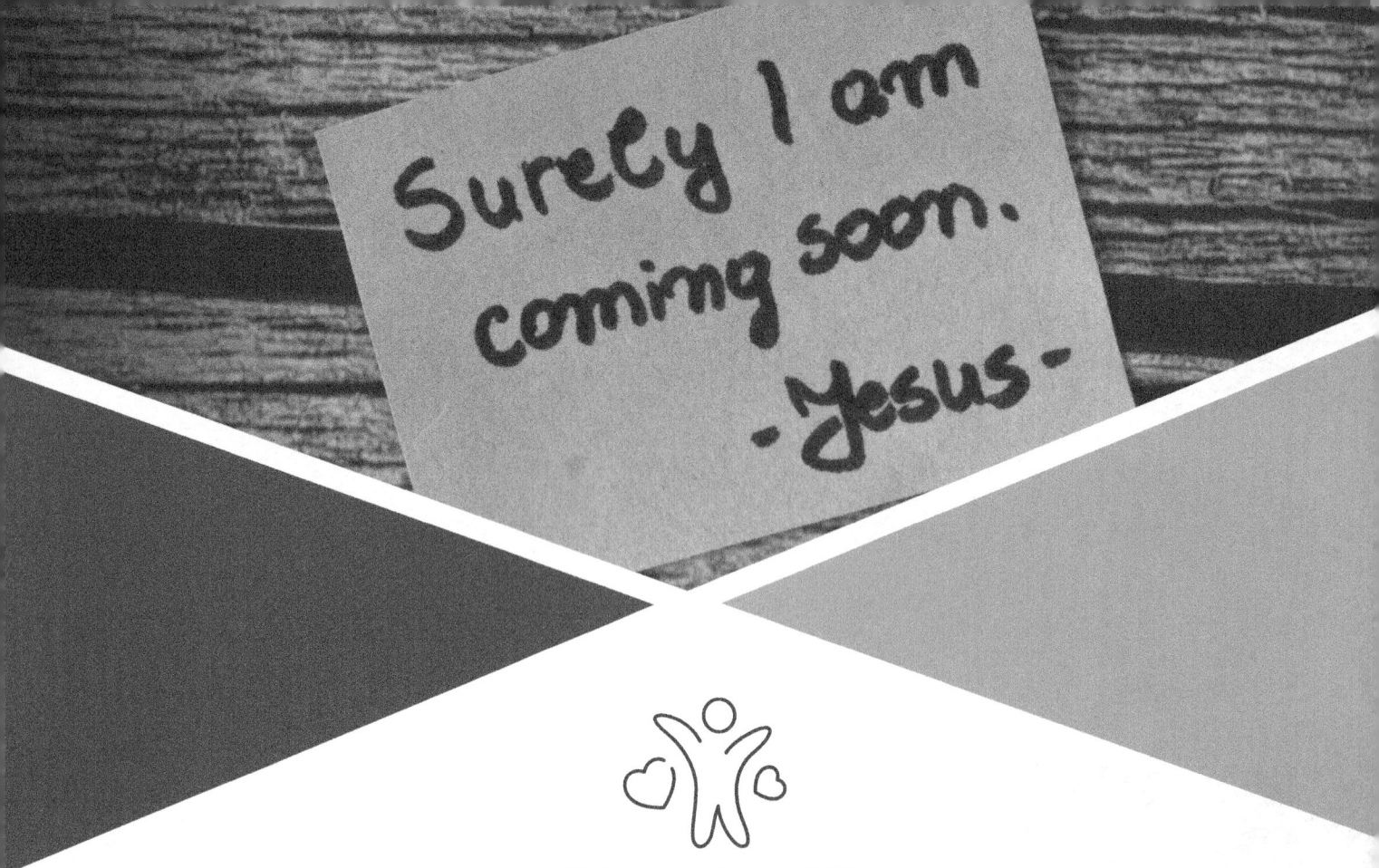

Chapter 27
The Joys & Promises of Evangelizing

In this chapter, you will find scriptural promises from God's Word that when a believer shares Christ with others it will bring them joy! In addition, God has promises waiting for the believer who will boldly and unashamedly step up and share Christ with the lost and backslidden. Read these Scriptures and allow them to prompt you to answer The Call of God to share Christ with others.

Daniel 12:3
And they that be wise shall shine as the brightness of the firmament; and they that turn many to righteousness as the stars for ever and ever.

Luke 15:6-7
And when he cometh home, he calleth together *his* friends and neighbours, saying unto them, Rejoice with me; for I have found my sheep which was lost. I say unto you, that likewise joy shall be in heaven over one sinner that repenteth, more than over ninety and nine just persons, which need no repentance.

John 4:34-36
Jesus saith unto them, My meat is to do the will of him that sent me, and to finish his work. Say not ye, There are yet four months, and *then* cometh harvest? behold, I say unto you, Lift up your eyes, and look on the fields; for they are white already to harvest. And he that reapeth receiveth wages, and gathereth fruit unto life eternal: that both he that soweth and he that reapeth may rejoice together.

Acts 15:3
And being brought on their way by the church, they passed through Phenice and Samaria, declaring the conversion of the Gentiles: and they caused great joy unto all the brethren.

1 Corinthians 3:6-9
I have planted, Apollos watered; but God gave the increase. So then neither is he that planteth any thing, neither he that watereth; but God that giveth the increase. Now he that planteth and he that watereth are one: and every man shall receive his own reward according to his own labour. For we are labourers together with God: ye are God's husbandry, ye are God's building.

Galatians 6:7
Be not deceived; God is not mocked: for whatsoever a man soweth, that shall he also reap.

Philippians 2:15-16
That ye may be blameless and harmless, the sons of God, without rebuke, in the midst of a crooked and perverse nation, among whom ye shine as lights in the world; Holding forth the word of life; that I may rejoice in the day of Christ, that I have not run in vain, neither laboured in vain.

James 5:19-20
Brethren, if any of you do err from the truth, and one convert him; Let him know, that he which converteth the sinner from the error of his way shall save a soul from death, and shall hide a multitude of sins.

Chapter 27
The Joys & Promises of Evangelizing

1. Write out Daniel 12:3 and speak it over yourself:

2. Write out the Scriptures, meditate on them, study them, and get the revelation settled into your spirit:

   a. James 5:19-20

   b. Philippians 2:15-16

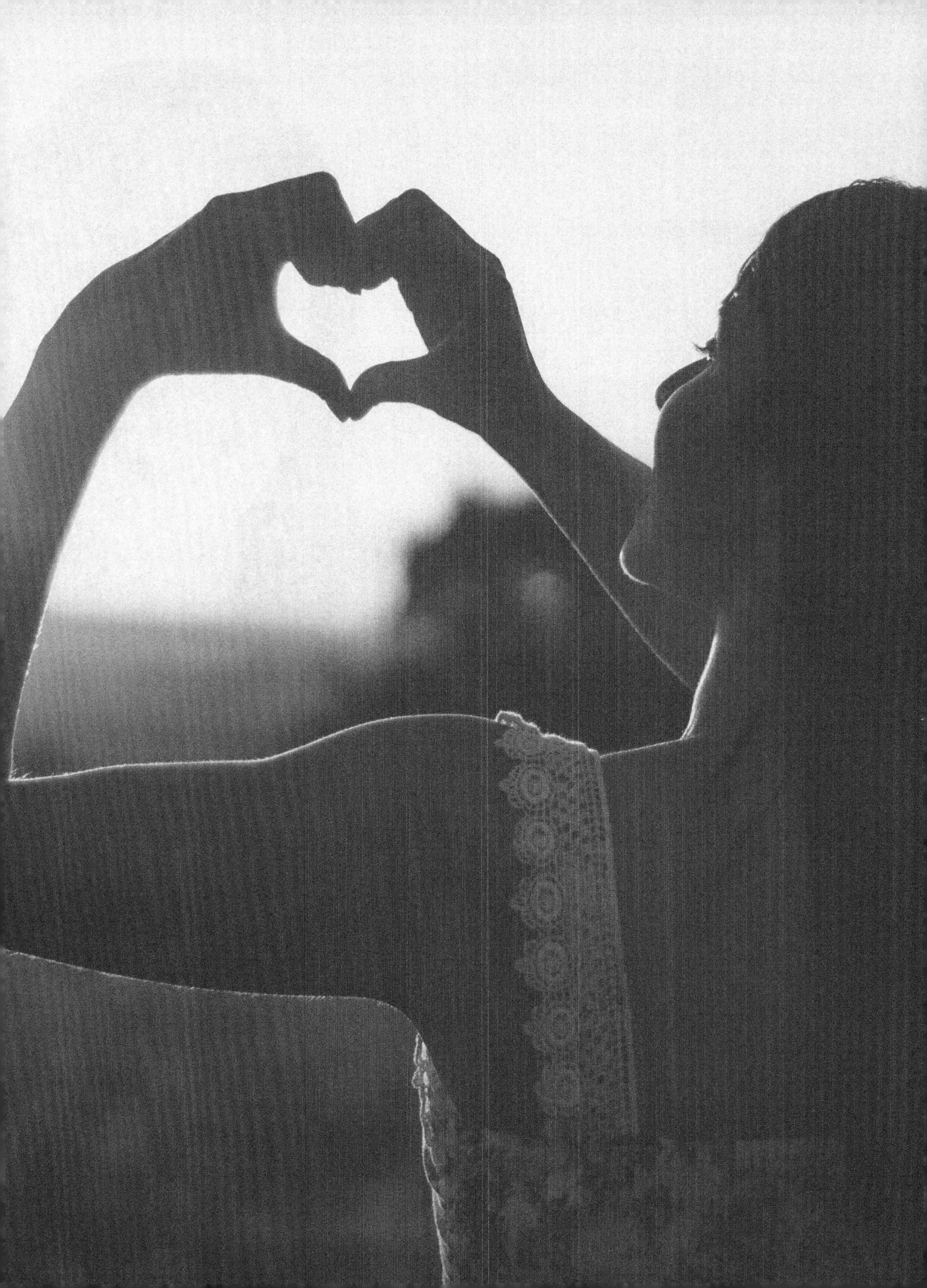

MARIE DIGGS
MINISTRIES

Closing Remarks

Look around. Can you see that we are living in the end of days? And guess what? God determined in His wisdom that you should live during this age. Therefore, as far as God is concerned, you are more than capable and able to carry out the Great Commission because you were born for such a time as this!

Yes! You have what it takes. So, yield your life to God completely, allow Him to fill you up with His Word and life, and pour you out onto the thirsty and dry people needing His love and provisions.

You will never know the full impact of your lifestyle of witnessing upon a person's life until you get to heaven. I pray that when you do get to heaven that you will be welcomed by Jesus and by a multitude of people who had the opportunity to taste God's goodness while living on the Earth, and who have the privilege of experiencing His everlasting love in heaven and throughout eternity!

"And this gospel of the kingdom shall be preached in all the world for a witness unto all nations; and then shall the end come" (Matthew 24:14).

Love you, and God bless you!

Marie K. Diggs, Evangelist

Author and Evangelist Marie Diggs

Since the age of five, Marie Diggs has known in her heart that God would use her to evangelize the nations.

Marie Diggs Ministries was started as a mandate from God to Marie and her husband, minister Marvin Diggs, to take the Gospel of Jesus Christ to the world. God has blessed Marie with opportunities to spread His Word throughout the United States, Canada, the Virgin Islands, Bulgaria, Poland, Southern India, the Czech Republic, and South Africa.

For almost 20 years, Marie served Word of Faith International Christian Center in Southfield, Michigan, in several leadership positions. Marie ministered the Healing Services and worked as staff Evangelist, Director of Outreach and Street Evangelism, and Director of the 24-Hour Prayer Center.

Today, Marie continues to inspire, equip, and empower the body of Christ domestically and abroad at Healing is Yours Conferences, Woman Rise Up Conferences, and at Answer the Call Be Bold Evangelism Training Classes. She also conducts a monthly A Night of Miracles Services, which is free to the public.

Marie and her husband reside in Michigan. Marie is available for speaking engagements. To learn more, visit *mariediggsministries.com/book-marie-diggs*

Answer the Call

be bold - evangelism workbook

Marie K. Diggs

MARIE DIGGS
MINISTRIES

P.O. Box 250471
West Bloomfield, MI 48325 • 248-990-0008
www.mariediggsministries.com

Copyright © 2023 Marie Diggs Ministries - All rights reserved.

Made in the USA
Monee, IL
20 April 2025